YES! You Can Land A Job
(Even) In A Crummy Economy

Published by Yours For The Dreaming
1501 Howard Avenue, Suite 203
Windsor, ON CANADA N8X 3T5

Printed In USA
For all general information contact Meet Therese at:
http://www.meettherese.com

DEDICATION

This book is dedicated to the memory of my Mom and Dad, Eleanor and Ed Smith, two people who really loved helping people they believed needed it most. Thank you, Mom, for teaching me the importance of being a good student. And thank you, Dad, for telling me that day as we walked into K-Mart that I could be whatever I wanted to be as long as I was willing to work for it.

Foreword

Over the past few years, alumna Therese Boldt has reached back to the Wayne State University School of Business Administration – energizing our Alumni Association and taking a concerted interest in the students who follow in her path. When Therese decided to write this book, *Yes! You Can Land A Job (Even) In A Crummy Economy*, I was delighted to offer the school's support. It is a timely and valuable resource for recent graduates and career veterans alike.

Within the book, Therese shares more than 20 years of experience in the recruiting industry, both as a top recruiter at one of the world's leading agencies and as founder of her own recruitment agency. At the School of Business Administration, our main goal is to prepare students for their professions. That entails not only theory and practice, but also the concepts Therese so aptly discusses in *Yes! You Can Land A Job (Even) In A Crummy Economy*, such as a positive, realistic attitude; self-knowledge; preparation; and perseverance.

In today's uncertain economy, our students are finding it more and more challenging to cross the commencement stage and step into their dream jobs. Throughout Therese's recruiting career, she has seen the ups and downs of our economy, with a particular focus on Southeastern Michigan. With that hindsight, she delivers an inspirational message: there is a job out there for you.

We were pleased to honor Therese with our Distinguished Alumna Award in 2007, in recognition of her distinction as a WSU Merit (now Presidential) Scholar and as a management major, her notable success as an entrepreneur, and her tireless efforts on behalf of our students and alumni. As president of the SBA Alumni Association, she has attracted a board of active business leaders; supported students through an endowed scholarship and joint efforts with the school's Career Planning and Placement Office; and helped reconnect us to alumni – some of whom have not been on campus in decades.

Therese's energy and commitment appear boundless. *Yes! You Can Land A Job (Even) In A Crummy Economy* is an extraordinary guide, but it is also evidence of the author's dedication to her alma mater and industry. I am confident the reader will derive great benefit from the book now and will want to use it as a reference throughout his or her career.

David L. Williams
Dean
Wayne State University School of Business Administration

ACKNOWLEDGMENTS

Over the course of the past several months, I have invested a huge amount of brain power on ideas to share with people who are looking for work. What can be done to help people who are in a state of panic about their occupational situation? Is it possible to create a resource that calms them down long enough to help them build some skills that will profoundly impact their careers and their lives? These thoughts kept me from enjoying my traditional eight hours of sleep many nights, but the creative tension brought on by the Michigan economy kept me moving forward. Now, I am happy to report that this first book is complete. And it could never have become a reality without the support of some very important people.

Reflecting on the support that I received from each of these individuals, a few common themes emerged. All of them have an undying belief in the possibility of things getting better. They also had an equally strong belief in my ability to inspire people through this book. Finally, they all encouraged me to act on that possibility. For that I am eternally grateful.

Thank you Dean David L. Williams, PhD and the entire team at the Wayne State University School of Business Administration. When I met with Dean Williams a few months ago to describe my vision of a practical book to help people get back to work, I wasn't sure how he would respond. (Having gotten good grades in college is one thing, but it is a far cry from being an academic!) It was, however, no surprise to learn he shared my vision of reaching out to our community at a time when help is most needed to transform careers and, as a result, transform our region.

Thank you John Agno, my coach, who hung in there with me throughout this process offering me the calm, safe space needed to sort things out on a weekly basis. You encouraged me to keep going even when tempted to stop, challenged me to slow down when moving too fast, helped me focus on what's important, and helped me learn how to tame the gremlins that emerged on this journey called success. The law of reciprocity states that if you want to create success for yourself, help someone else become successful. If you type "law of reciprocity" into Google, you will get 3,190,000 search results. The very first one is a link to John's site. Need I say more?

Kay Douglas, my friend, my confidante, my marketing guru and my champion. There is no way this book would have gotten into the hands of the people who need it had you not stepped up and taken on the challenge. At a time when you surely had more important fish to fry, you and your team at Douglas Marketing Group artistically crafted my message into a format that will keep readers engaged in the process of moving forward in their job search. Thank you, my friend, from the bottom of my heart.

Thank you Elizabeth Rackover, my assistant, my friend, and the person who painstakingly looked over each chapter as it was completed to make sure that readers would understand what the heck I was trying to say. Your perspective, gentle candor, and especially your loyal commitment to this book's vision are truly appreciated. I am happy and grateful to have you share in this experience, that is, for me, a profound "mark of in between" where I lay down vanishing and woke up golden. Thank you.

Kenton Smith, my brother, and editor-in-chief. Thank you for the hours that you (and Evelyn) spent meticulously proofreading each chapter, paragraph, word, and punctuation mark. Your gift of attention to detail is not one that I possess, but it is certainly one that is appreciated. Thank you for making this book acceptable from a grammatical perspective…even if I do like to use three dots…a lot!

The act of writing is not a team sport. It required a fair amount of alone time at the PC…time not spent with the family I love so much. But because they shared my vision, they gave me the space needed to create. Fred, thank you, my love, for your unwavering faith in me and in my ability to bring my dream to fruition (and for putting up with the click of the keyboard when you tried to get much needed sleep!).

Finally, to my daughter, Alexa – thank you for writing that poem in 4th grade which ended with these lines:
"I dream that I am an author
        I am trying to write a book
 I hope to have a million dollars
        I am wonderful and creative."

I appreciate each of you more than you will ever know.

Table of Contents

introduction

Every successful recruiter has what is known as a desk specialty. They build their reputation on knowing a particular industry or niche and by developing relationships that glean optimum results for a hiring company.

If you are a job seeker, the numbers are not typically in your favor when working with a recruiter. You see, for each person who gets hired, 3-4 other people have been interviewed and eliminated. For each person who has interviewed with the hiring company, the recruiter has probably interviewed 3-5 candidates. (We're at anywhere from 12:1 to 25:1 odds now.) For each person the recruiter has interviewed in person, he or she has probably phone-screened 10-20 applicants. (Our numbers are getting steeper now; we're at 120:1 to 500:1.) And finally, for each person phone-screened, the recruiter has probably reviewed 25-30 resumes and eliminated all but one, so our numbers have become staggering. Best case, you have a 1-in-3,000 chance of getting hired when using the services of a professional recruiter; worst case is 1 in 15,000. And yet we tell our candidates (and I believe this) that their odds of landing a job are better using us than simply responding to an Internet ad.

I have been a part of the recruiting industry since 1987. For over 20 years I have felt a certain sense of guilt about not being able to help everyone who calls me looking for a job. For every opening I fill, there are about 9,000 people who didn't get hired but still want to find a job. Being true to my Catholic upbringing it was important to satisfy my well honed guilt mechanism by developing a tool that will help those people who were not placed in a job.

This book was written with these people in mind. It is for all of you who did not get the job. My reward is to see you land happily in a job that is enriching or rewarding or whatever you want it to be. My commitment is to give you a valuable resource, and that means:

The concepts are easy to grasp

The language is easy to read and understand

The content is relevant and easily applied

The book can be read in one weekend

The font is big and there's lots of white space

There are pictures and/or graphs that you don't need an advanced degree to understand

So, my hope is that I have achieved "valuable resource" status in your eyes too.

Here goes...

traditional *methods* of looking for a *job*

Chapter 1

I don't need to spend a lot of time on how people typically look for a job. You've probably used these tactics yourself. But if you are one of the rare few who have found themselves safely in the employ of one company for the majority of your career, I'll give a few brief descriptions of how people usually go about conducting a career search – based, of course, on what I've heard.

1

I Look In The Classified Ads

Yes, there are still advertisements in the classified section of most newspapers, and yes, there are still people who read them. When people read them they are motivated either to find a job or to "see what's out there." Both of these people aren't really getting what they think they're getting. We'll talk about using this as a method to find a job later on, but using the classifieds to see "what's out there" is about as effective as standing on the top of the Empire State Building to see what the United States looks like. You'll get a view of what's within your eyeshot, but you won't see the whole picture. After all, it might be a cloudy day, or you may be in need of a new eyeglass prescription, or God forbid, it might be nighttime. In any event, the classifieds are a method to find a job, but don't fool yourself into believing they are the only or best way to find a job. Know their limitations.

I Look For Openings Posted On The Internet

Also known as the "electronic classifieds," the Internet when used to find a job or "see what's out there" has its limitations too. Again, we'll talk about using this method to look for a job later, but using the Internet to "see what's out there" is as effective as flying a jet from NY to LA in order to see what the United States looks like. You'll get a great overview and see a lot of cool things, but the details will be blurry and you can't likely land in any one place without the fear of crashing. (We'll talk about posting your resume on line.)

I Am Working With A Recruiter

Recruiters (good ones) can help you in a number of ways, but as I said earlier, if you use a recruiter you have to understand their limitations. For instance, recruiters work specific desks; and if your area of experience or expertise lies outside the recruiter's specialty, they will not be able to help land you a position. Also, understand that good recruiters (like those good companies you'd like to work for) are being contacted by hundreds of other people who are in the same boat as you. So sending your carefully crafted cover letter and resume will likely have the same result as sending your information to a good company you'd like to work for.

I Send My Resume To Companies I'd Like To Work For

Some people will actually be somewhat proactive and contact companies they have an interest in working for, based upon things they've heard about the company's reputation or based upon their perception of the company's success or track record. If you are one of these folks, you will normally craft a cover letter that seems to address what you assume might be important to the company on the receiving end, attach a clean copy of your most up-to-date resume, and send it off to someone (usually HR) who doesn't have a clue who you are or why they should hire you. Your carefully crafted resume is dutifully logged in with the other 800-80,000 resumes from people who have the same idea about "getting their foot in the door," and then placed "ON FILE" for whatever amount of time the law says the company needs to retain such records. From my experience, I can assure you that once your resume is placed "ON FILE" your chances of it ever being looked at again are about the same as being hit by a meteor while you're in your hot tub.

I Have My Resume Posted Online

Posting your resume online and hoping to get a hit is a popular method for landing a job. It works like this: You find one or a hundred posting sites - the bigger the better too! - and you post your resume. You declare what you want to do, where you want to do it, and what you have done. You then assume that the right company that has the right opening for you sees your beautifully crafted resume (while they are reviewing several thousand others) and selects yours as the most qualified.

This presents a few problems.

How are you positioned in relationship to other applicants?

Who is reading the site?

Confidentiality.

This idea of confidentiality brings up another tactic some job seekers employ when posting their resumes online. I talk to lots of people who don't want their boss to know they are looking for a new job, so they leave off any information that can link them to their current employer - like their name, the company they work for, and the companies they used to work for. OK, let's put ourselves for a minute in the shoes of an HR person who might stumble onto this type of resume.

Their **first** question is, **"whose resume am I looking at?"** Not sure.

Their **second** question is, **"where does this person work?"** No answer.

Their **third** question is, **"why did they leave off this information?"**

Are you getting the picture?

If someone gets to a third unanswerable question, it is almost guaranteed that your resume will be placed **"ON FILE,"** and we've already discussed what happens to those resumes.

You see, if your resume raises questions, it is allowing the receiving party to make assumptions. And we all know that when you have to rely on another person's assumptions, you're getting into dangerous territory.

Chapter 2

I remember, back when I was in college, hearing the term "networking." At that time of my life, the word networking brought the following image to mind: I'm in a room full of people who I don't know, who I probably don't want to know, and I am most likely talking about things I'm not interested in. My goal of this endeavor is to convince people that I am worthy of them doing something for me that will further my goals. In essence, networking meant selling me to a bunch of people who may or not be interested in buying me.

In all my years of recruiting, when I have asked someone involved in a job search how they were going about landing a new job, seldom was their first response, "I'm networking." Yet, using your network is probably the most effective way to land a job. In fact, studies show that nearly 70% of all positions are filled through a referral. And referrals happen through networking. But most networking fails because the networker (jobseeker) isn't really tapping into the right people; and if they are, they are most likely not sending the right message. What do I mean?

Tapping Into The Right People

Who do you think needs to know about your job search? There's a logical group of people who can likely help you. Let's pinpoint the basics and then broaden our reach.

People who know you socially (family, friends, neighbors, etc.)

People who know you professionally
(most current boss, coworkers, etc.)

People who knew you professionally
(previous boss, coworkers, etc.)

People who do what you do

People who work with people like you

People to whom people like you report

People who hire people like you

People who associate with people like you

Wayne Baker, in his book *Achieving Success Through Social Capital*, suggests that it's not who you know but rather *who knows you*. So what does this mean in the life of a job seeker? It's very unlikely that your immediate network (family, friends, neighbors) will land you a job. You're not going to come home one day after receiving your pink slip, ask your mom or dad what to do and get very far. It's doubtful that these supportive and well-meaning people will know about an employer who needs someone just like you right at this very moment. It is, however, likely that the people who your immediate network knows (your network's network) could very well lead you closer to your goal of finding a new job.

A Real-Life Networking Story

I'll demonstrate how networking has worked in my recruiting practice. You see, I, like you, am always looking for a job. I recently filled a position supporting the CEO of a very prominent not-for-profit organization in Southeastern Michigan. It was a textbook example of the ideal position for me to fill: The CEO's executive assistant of 10 years was retiring. They had tried to find a replacement (using the traditional methods of hiring; advertising, using a recruiter, and tapping into their referral network) and nothing had worked.

As the employer tapped into his network though, my name came up. He didn't know me. I didn't know him. But someone he knew, knew someone who knew me. His network's network connected with my network's network. So I began to work on the search.

Next, my job was to find the right candidate. Again I tapped into my network, and found a candidate with exactly the right qualifications and experience. And guess what? It turns out that this candidate's former boss was a part of my client's network. Ultimately, it wasn't just her qualifications that got her the job, and it wasn't who she knew; it was who knew her.

Sending The Right Message

We'll talk later in more depth about the message that will get you closer to your next position. You've heard of the 60-second elevator speech? For now, let's talk about the common message most job seekers send out. It goes something like this:

> " Hi, John. I'm not sure if you heard this, but I just got laid off from ABC. "

This opening statement by you is followed by a litany of injustices you have endured which are then validated by your friend John (who, by the way, is very empathetic and knows other people who are in the same boat). He knows that times are tough, and he is ready to jump onto the "it sucks that you no longer have a job" bandwagon.

Once this mutual moment of despair is over, you (the job seeker) ask, "Do you know anyone who's hiring?" Think about it... John has read the papers and listened to the evening news. In his worldview, no one is hiring. And if by chance John *does* know of someone who is hiring, it's certain they won't be hiring someone like you.

You leave this networking conversation feeling pretty deflated, and certainly not motivated to make another networking connection. Or worse yet, you pick up the phone and make similar calls to other people you know, just to get similar responses.

Not very positive is it?

So Is There A Better Approach?

I think so. But it begins with a positive statement. It dwells on who you are and what your vision is rather than leading with the current reality (layoff) that begets further negativity regarding your job search. How about this:

" Hi, John, I'm not sure if you heard this, but I'm involved in a career search. "

This statement is followed by a glimpse at your vision for your career and the direction you are headed in. Your follow-up or closing question goes something like this:

" Who do you know who I might connect with to discuss my career goals further? "

Different approach, huh? This question doesn't require the other person to know anything about the job market, your position or your profession. It only requires this person to make a decision about whether or not he or she knows someone you can talk with. It's not threatening. It requires no special knowledge. And it leaves you not deflated, but with a sense of forward momentum and brighter possibilities.

become
your own
Professional Recruiter

Chapter 3

Landing a job in a crummy
economy requires you to go at
an old problem using new tools.
Remember the old adage,
"if you keep doin' what you're
doin', then you'll keep gettin'
what you're gettin'" ? If you
want to land a job, you'll have
to take control of your search.

So How Can You Take Control Of Your Job Search?

What is a more active approach that will give you results rather than rejection? You can become your own Professional Recruiter. Rather than waiting for the right opportunity to arise, you can take matters into your own hands and go out after the career of your dreams. Successful recruiters are not the people sitting in pretty offices waiting for the phone to ring. They are the people who, during economically challenging times, make things happen. They get busy and get active, and guess what? They don't have time to dwell on the possibility of slow times because, after all, they are busy creating momentum.

What Does A Professional Recruiter Do?

A Professional Recruiter:

> *Establishes* **who** the product is.
>
> *Determines* **where** to market the product.
>
> *Determines* **how** to connect with the person who will hire you.

Then he or she:

> *Develops* a **pitch** or **presentation.**
>
> *Sets* a **goal** for each call.
>
> *Sets* a daily or weekly **activity goal.**
>
> *Measures* and *records* the **results.**

Establishing Who The Product Is

I'll never forget my first day as an account executive with what was then the world's largest recruiting firm. I was asked to sit in a conference room with another trainee (they called us rookies) and watch videotapes that would turn us into successful headhunters. The first lesson was about the product we would be taking to market: the MPC.

The MPC – The Product

During my strenuous training period as a recruiter, I was told the quickest way to make a placement was to place your MPC - your Most Placeable Candidate. Back in the day, many recruiters would read the want ads and call the companies who had posted openings in them to learn if the positions were filled. Some would send resumes to companies they wanted to represent in hopes that the company would want to work with them. Others still would blindly fax resumes to companies they knew experienced turnover in certain positions. But, the most successful recruiters knew the best way to make a placement was to place their MPC.

you can **be** the MPC
Most Placeable Candidate

But What's An MPC?

An MPC, by definition:

> has **marketable** skills/talents
>
> is **motivated** to accept a new position
>
> has **realistic expectations** on money, benefits, etc.
>
> is **reference-checkable**
>
> is **willing** to work in a **cooperative** vein

So why is this method so effective? Let's look at why the "other" ways are not. Calling companies who have placed an ad are much like calling to inquire about a home for sale in a healthy housing market. By the time the listing hits the press, several people have toured the home, and at least one prospect has probably made an offer. When I bought my first home in 1993 (a very robust period of time in the housing industry in Michigan), my realtor called the glossy advertisements that came in the weekend paper "sold" listing. Similarly, by the time you read an advertisement in the classified ads for an opening, many prospective candidates have been considered. In fact, the hiring game is such a time-sensitive process that it is quite possible a posted position will be filled even before the ad appears in the paper.

In the 80's and 90's when my recruiting career was leaping forward at light speed, I remember candidates complaining that they thought recruiters were placing ads for positions that did not exist. These job seekers would answer an ad placed by a recruiter, and show up for the interview only to find that the position advertised had already been filled. The resourceful recruiter would then explain to the applicant that she would be considered for other positions available, but the applicant would leave the recruiting office feeling tricked. It's the old bait and switch. But was it a bait and switch? I suppose there were some less scrupulous recruiters who were capable of falsely advertising, but for the most part, I believe these scenarios were a matter of timing.

Let's break it down. An employer has an opening occur on Monday. They write an ad on Tuesday. Deadline for the paper is Wednesday. Paper is released on Sunday. You respond on Monday. That's nearly a week between the time the employer experiences the opening and the time you hear about it and respond. Think about the employer's state of mind when they realize they need to hire someone. They are *very* motivated to find someone. (Not too different from your state of mind when you realize you need to find a job!) They are going to talk to everyone they know, dedicate every available moment, and use every possible resource they can get their hands on to fill this opening. They are not going to wait to fill the position until the ad runs to see if the ideal candidate happens to fall into their laps. Recruiters are no different. When the right person comes along, the deal is done. But let's assume the opening is still viable when the advertisement runs.

Why isn't sending your resume the most effective way to get that job ?

Why don't successful recruiters use this method to land their candidates a job?

Why Sending Resumes Just Isn't Effective

It's really a matter of odds. It's a numbers thing. If you send your resume in response to an advertisement, you are one of many applicants - sometimes hundreds! - who are doing the very same thing. These, in my opinion, aren't good odds. Hoping my resume is more attractive than 300 others is not something I can hang my hat on. Am I saying not to send your resume? No. I am only explaining that in doing so, the odds are greater that your resume will be rejected than accepted so use other search methods too.

What about simply faxing or emailing your resume to companies you think would be great employers?

While this method may appear to be proactive, it does have a few flaws.
Let's take a look:

To whom within the company should you send your resume? Unless you have been given the name of the individual who is responsible for hiring someone just like you, you are making an assumption. And when you make an assumption, there is a 50/50 chance of being wrong.

How do you best present your credentials? Unless you have a clear understanding of what's important to the individual who is reading your resume, you are making an assumption. And, again there is a 50/50 chance you will make the wrong choice in presenting your strengths.

How do you follow up? Unless you fully understand what the company's process is for considering candidates for hire, you are making an assumption that following up is okay. If you follow up, and how you follow up, exposes you to the 50/50 chance that it's unwelcome or unneeded communication that will eliminate your chances of being hired.

We will talk later about using your resume as a marketing tool. But for now, you'll need to trust me that this method of presenting your experience and talent to an employer (who doesn't know you) will most likely get your resume placed in the electronic recycle bin or, at more traditional firms, in File 13.

I hope I am making a compelling argument for you to try something that worked extremely well for me for many, many years. Just to refresh your memory, I filled clerical positions - positions that were traditionally NOT filled by recruiters. Employers hired me (actually paid me thousands of dollars) to find clerical employees who earned $7 …$8… $9 per hour during a time when "no one was hiring" and where applicants were told "the competition is tough because so many people are out of work."

And during these "tough times," I consistently out-produced recruiters across the country who operated in significantly less challenged metropolitan areas.

How Did I Do It? I started with the right mindset.

success starts with the right mindset

Chapter 4

As in any endeavor, before you take the first step, you need to make sure you are in the right frame of mind. Athletes do it. Performers do it. Business and political leaders do it. They envision the goal – success – before they take action. Looking for a job, especially in a crummy economy, is no different.

Changing My Perspective

As I navigated through the recession of the early 1990's, I refused to accept things at face value. I refused to buy into the bad news that my competitors, potential clients and candidates wanted to talk about. When people would complain about the bad economy, I would say, "I have chosen not to participate in the bad economy." I admit, people looked at me as if I had lost my mind. But, thought precedes action. If my thoughts were focused on how "bad" things were, those bad things would continue to happen. You've read the books: what you think about becomes your reality. I chose to think about getting busy placing people - despite the "bad" economy.

Creating The Need

Did you know thousands of people are hired for jobs that didn't exist before they interviewed? Sounds crazy, doesn't it? In my recruiting practice, I experienced this phenomenon many times. I would talk to an employer about the features and benefits of a great candidate with whom I had met, and they would agree to meet that person despite the fact there was no opening. Why? There could be a few reasons:

The employer knows about an opening that is soon to occur;

Maybe an employee has indicated that he or she will be leaving, but the employer has not yet started the recruiting process;

The employer is dissatisfied with someone who currently holds the position but doesn't want to go to the trouble of initiating a search yet;

The employer is thinking about restructuring or reorganizing the staff, and a candidate like the one I have described might fit nicely.

You see, all of these scenarios are possible. And guess what? You as the job seeker won't necessarily know about them unless you consider these possibilities and attempt to "Create the Need." When I stopped looking for openings and began to look for opportunities to create openings, my success increased tremendously.

Handling Objections

I got better at handling the objections employers and candidates gave me. I had a trainer share a few great phrases with me.

The first phrase was,

> An objection is simply your invitation to sell or offer more information.

Objections are many times made as an automatic response. Think about it. You walk into a clothing store because you need a new pair of blue jeans. A nice young lady approaches you and asks, "Can I help you?" What do you say in response 99% of the time? "No thank you. I'm just looking." Of course you're just looking, but that wasn't the question. The question really was, "How can I help make this experience more pleasant for you?" But shoppers - or clients, or potential employers - all have programmed responses to nearly all questions that are pitched to them. And if you can move past the programmed responses, you can oftentimes have conversations that will build the types of relationships that will help the other person help you get to the job opportunity of your dreams. Let's look at an example:

Candidate:	"I'm looking for a job, and I'm wondering if you can help me?"
Employer:	"Sure, but we don't have any openings."

The employer has just given you a conditioned response because he or she has been inundated with job seekers who say, "I'm looking for a job, and I'm wondering if you have any openings." He has tuned you out as soon as he hears the words "I'm looking for a job" and fills in the rest of the sentence with the words he's heard time and time again. So what can you do to move beyond the conditioned response? Let's continue the conversation:

Candidate:	"I understand that you don't have any openings, but I would really like to learn more about what you and your company look for in _____ (fill in the blank with whatever your line of work is) when you do hire."

Notice what you've done? You've acknowledged that the employer cannot hire you at the moment, but you have moved into a fact-finding mode that may pay off for you in a couple of ways. First, you may gather useful information that will help you position yourself in the best possible light with a similar company (who may actually need someone like you!). OR you may get the employer thinking about what it takes to make a great candidate for a _____ position (and just maybe you have those traits!) OR at the very least, you have taken the next step in building a relationship with a hiring manager (who, by the way, knows many other managers who could be looking for someone just like you!). Just by moving beyond the reflex answer the employer has given you, you now have three potential openings for forward movement.

The second great phrase was,

> ❝ 'No' is the second best answer. ❞

Most people, when they hear the word "no," feel rejected. "They don't want me." "I'm not good enough." But to the contrary, "no" is simply the second best answer. As you look for a job, you'll come to appreciate "no" rather than dread it. You see, for every "no" you hear you are one step closer to a "yes." Have you ever heard the story about

Colonel Sanders? He heard "no" 1008 times before he heard "yes" from a restaurant willing to use his Kentucky Fried Chicken recipe. What kept him going? His undying belief that what he had to offer was something of value. What can keep you going in your search? The undying belief that what you have to offer is something of value: you and your talents. So rather than stopping at the natural response you feel when you hear "no," try remembering that "no" is simply the second best response, and take a moment to consider that you are one step closer to the "yes" that will land you in your next job.

And the last great phrase was,

> "Forever means for now."

This was a tough one for me. I have a great memory, and when someone says they don't want something, I believe they will never want it. It took me some time to realize that even though a hiring manager may never want to use a recruiter to hire a secretary, one day, circumstances may be such that he has to tap into the very resource he never imagined using. This same principle holds true outside the hiring paradigm too. I remember when I was about 10 years old, I watched my sisters apply mascara. It looked like a lot of work, and I was sure I'd poke my eye out if I ever tried to apply it. I said to them, "I'll never wear mascara!" Forever meant for now. Once circumstances changed (puberty hit), and I realized the benefit of making my eyelashes look longer (peer pressure), what I thought I would never do became a daily routine. So when someone tells you "we never hire people with this background" or "we only hire people with that background," they are telling you what is true - not forever, but for now. Keep in mind that the door may open for you when the situation is right.

In the search for your next position, you will become your Most Placeable Candidate. And you will become the recruiter who will make that placement happen. And guess what? You'll probably get even better results than a recruiter would, because you aren't charging the hiring client a fee!

But where do you start? Let's look at the characteristics of an MPC.

YOU ARE
YOUR MPC
Most Placeable Candidate

Chapter 5

If you are ready to land a job, that is if you are ready to place your MPC (you), you'll need to put yourself to the test to determine if you truly are a Most Placeable Candidate. Successful recruiters – the ones who successfully navigate the rough waters of a down economy – know that the fastest way to a placement is to place their MPC. But what does it take to be an MPC?

An MPC Has Marketable Skills & Talents

If you are going to place yourself effectively and be your own agent of record, you'll need to know your product. Any successful recruiter will market only candidates who have marketable skills or talents.

what are your **strengths**?

what are you *really* **good at**?

what are your **weaknesses**?

what areas do you *need* to **improve**?

How many of us really spend much time understanding what our core competencies are? Face it: from the time we were teenagers, we've probably spent more time thinking about what's wrong with us than what is right with us. When you begin a job search, it's time to reveal what you are really good at and acknowledge (not dwell on) what your weaknesses are. No need to beat up on yourself unnecessarily, just put it all down on paper.

When I decided to rebrand my coaching practice - which is very much like changing jobs! - I did an exercise that helped me really understand what I was good at and what I needed to improve, as well as identify what opportunities were possible, along with potential threats to my success in making the change. The exercise is called a SWOT (**S**trengths, **W**eaknesses, **O**pportunities, **T**hreats) Analysis. Companies do SWOT analyses all the time to help them move forward, so why not use the same tool on the company called, "Me: The Job Seeker?"

The following table summarizes the components of a SWOT Analysis:

What Are My Greatest **STRENGTHS?**	What Are My Greatest **WEAKNESSES?**
What do I do well? What am I really good at? What advantages do I have? What relevant resources do I have access to? What do other people see as my strengths? Consider this from your own point of view and from the point of view of the people you deal with. Don't be modest – but DO be realistic. If you are having any difficulty with this, try writing down a list of your characteristics. Some of these will hopefully be strengths! In looking at your strengths, think about them in relation to your competitors – the people who you will be competing with for a particular job.	What am I not so good at? What could I improve? Again, consider this from both an internal and external perspective: Do other people seem to perceive weaknesses that you do not see? Are your competitors doing any better than you? It is best to be realistic now, and face any unpleasant truths as soon as possible.

What OPPORTUNITIES Are There For Me?

Where are these good opportunities?

What interesting business or employment trends am I aware of?

What opportunities might there be to transfer my skills & experience into a new line of work?

Opportunities can come from such things as changes in technology, changes in government policy, changes in social patterns, population profiles, lifestyle changes, etc. A useful approach to looking at opportunities is to look at your strengths and ask yourself whether these strengths open up any opportunities. Alternatively, look at your weaknesses and ask yourself whether you could open up opportunities by eliminating them. Get creative!

What Are The Potential THREATS To My Success?

What obstacles do I face?

What is my competition doing?

Are my requirements changing?

Carrying out this analysis will often be illuminating - both in terms of pointing out what needs to be done, and in putting problems into perspective.

NOW you fill in the blanks...

WHAT ARE MY GREATEST STRENGTHS?

WHAT ARE MY GREATEST WEAKNESSES?

WHAT OPPORTUNITIES ARE THERE FOR ME?

WHAT ARE THE POTENTIAL THREATS TO MY SUCCESS?

Is this exercise overwhelming?

Is it tough for you to take time to put yourself
under the microscope?

Are you having a hard time getting started?

If so, why not ask your friends, coworkers, bosses, mentors, family… anyone close to
you… to help. As I mentioned earlier, when I changed my brand, I had a tough time
starting this process. So I asked about 30 people who knew me to answer the four
SWOT questions in the table above. I went one step further, and asked them to send
their responses to my coach (a third party) so they knew their responses would be
held in confidence. If you don't have a coach (which I'm guessing you don't if you're
unemployed) why not ask someone you trust and who cares about you to compile
the responses you receive. You will be amazed at what you learn about yourself: the
strengths people see that you didn't think were important, the opportunities that you
never considered as possibilities.

An MPC Is Motivated To Accept A New Position

Successful recruiters work only with candidates who are truly motivated to make a job
change. What's motivating you besides the fact that you may not be employed?

In my recruiting practice, I spent countless hours helping candidates see beyond their
immediate need for a job. We would take time to look at what was working in their
last jobs, and what wasn't working in their last jobs. Then we'd use this information
to identify what their motivators were. Usually, what was important was related to the
following factors:

Challenge – How challenging is the position? Does it draw on your talents? Does it include the responsibilities that really light you up? Can you see yourself doing the job and truly enjoying it?

Advancement – How fast or how far will you advance within the company? How long will it take to get to the next position? Is your definition of advancement upward mobility? Or does advancement mean professional or personal growth? Or is it expanded responsibilities?

Security – How secure is the position? How financially secure is the company or the industry? Is the future predictable?

Money – How much money will you make now? And what is the possibility for monetary growth? What types of benefits are offered? How is performance rewarded?

Location – If you are involved in a local job search, how far are you willing to drive? (In the metropolitan Detroit area, the commuting professional tends to look for positions within 45 minutes of his or her home.) If you are willing to relocate, what areas are most acceptable? What are least acceptable?

Environment – What type of environment or culture will your next job be in? This includes not just the physical surroundings, but the corporate climate, the relationships with superiors, peers and others. (In my business - placing the executive secretary to the CEO - the chemistry between the executive and the assistant is almost always the top priority for both parties.)

On the next page, you will find an inventory or checklist that breaks down each of these categories.

Career Check-up

Rate each statement using the rating scale described below.

5=Strongly agree   **4**=Agree   **3**=Neither Agree nor Disagree   **2**=Disagree   **1**=Strongly Disagree

Ask yourself about CHALLENGE…
My job is more challenging today than it was a year ago.
I feel I am adding value to my company/department/division.
My superiors are aware of the value I am adding.
My job allows me to be innovative and creative.
I feel empowered in my current position.

Ask yourself about ADVANCEMENT…
My current position allows for advancement opportunities.
I am kept informed of both advancement opportunities and lateral moves.
My position involves continuous learning opportunities.
I can keep abreast of trends and technological advancements that make me more marketable.
My manager encourages continuing education.
My company supports continuing education by offering tuition assistance.

Ask yourself about SECURITY…
My company has a solid plan for ongoing growth and financial success.
My company is financially strong.
Turnover is low within my company (i.e. no recent layoffs/tenure is high).
My company's vision is to stay ahead of the competition and is meeting that goal.
My manager is committed to my success and my position within the company.

Ask yourself about ENVIRONMENT…
The overall tone of my office is very positive and team oriented.
My coworkers share my level of commitment in producing quality work.
I have faith in our management team and support its decisions.
My company is well organized with consistent policies and procedures.
Management treats all employees fairly and with respect.
The physical environment is aesthetically pleasing (i.e. clean, organized, technologically advanced).

Ask yourself about LOCATION…
The commute to my office is less than 45 minutes one way.
My office is not planning to relocate within the next year.
My office is located in a safe area.
I do not plan to move my residence within the next year.

Ask yourself about MONEY…
My compensation is adequate as compared to others within my classification.
My performance is reviewed regularly and is based upon measurable criteria.
Raises in my company are comparable to those given within my industry.
I have maintained the same level of fringe benefits in the last year.

TOTAL _____

What Your Score Could Mean:
135 - 150 Points › You seem to be in the right place
120 - 134 Points › There may be some areas that need attention
105 - 119 Points › You may be feeling some job dissatisfaction
90 - 104 Points › Your career may not be heading in the right direction
≤ 75 Points › You are most likely not in the right job for you

An MPC Has Realistic Expectations About Money & Benefits

In the recruiting business, if you are going to make placements, you'll do well to only represent candidates who are realistic about the amount of money they will accept in a new position. The last thing a recruiter wants to see is an offer turned down because a candidate is being unrealistic about salary expectations.

But what is realistic? There are many opinions surrounding the topic of what a person can realistically expect to earn when he or she accepts a new position. I'll talk later about salary negotiations, but for now let's talk about some common opinions:

I always inflate my earnings.

I've heard this statement made by many people in the job search mode. These people believe that the best way to get more money is to lie. After all, everyone else does, don't they? The answer is no. Misrepresenting your earnings isn't a good way to begin the relationship with your new employer. And oftentimes, if you make such a misrepresentation on paper, and the real facts are revealed, you've made a solid case for your immediate termination.

I prefer not to tell an employer how much I make.

Some people choose to avoid the topic altogether. This too creates a problem. First, an employer can (and usually will) find out how much you earn. It's a matter of public record. Second, avoiding the question is giving a potential employer the opportunity to start questioning your motives or worse yet drawing their own conclusions based upon their reality.

I deserve to make more.

While I believe we should all strive to make more, and most of us are deserving, this logic doesn't work with employers.

I haven't gotten a raise in 4 years.

The fact of the matter is that in a down economy, many companies offer incentives that are not tied to compensation. You are not in the minority if you haven't received a raise. Be careful, though, not to cast a doubtful shadow onto your performance. Is there a reason you haven't gotten a raise?

In the last 20 years of my recruiting life, I have found that when making a job change, a person can anticipate receiving a salary offer that lies in a range between his or her current salary to about 10% more. I'm not saying people don't get 20-25% raises, but it is very rare, and there are most likely some extenuating circumstances (e.g., higher risk) that drive a hiring company to provide more money up front in an offer. Usually, though, if a hiring company wants to entice someone monetarily, it will take the form of a one-time signing bonus and not an inflated starting wage.

An MPC Is Reference-Checkable

If a recruiter cannot verify your employment at the very least and learn more about your character at most, he will likely not represent you. When selecting an MPC, a recruiter will check a candidate's references not only to verify information, but to learn things that can be used in the selling process.

Who will vouch for you? And more importantly, what will they say about you? I have interviewed hundreds of people who spend little time cultivating references. These are the people who leave jobs and never turn back. When asked who can vouch for their effectiveness, etc., they will shrug their shoulders and say, "I don't know who's at the company anymore. I don't keep in touch with anyone from there." I say, shame on you. When you leave an employer, think of the people with whom you have built relationships during your tenure. As you leave, gather their contact information, and obtain letters of recommendation or at least their commitment to speak on your behalf in the future. Then stay in touch with them! These people are a key to your continued success.

Another thing I hear from candidates is, "I don't know what he'll say about me." This is dangerous. An employer who is considering hiring you will talk with this person (sometimes at length) and learn many things about you and how you operate. You need to have an inkling of what types of comments will be made. How do you find that out? ASK! Ask your former boss/peer/subordinate what they feel your greatest strengths are. What they really relied on you for. What your reputation was. What areas you need to develop. What type of job they think you would be most suited for. Open up a dialog to determine if there are red flags. If you are hearing negatives, you can be assured your potential next employer will hear them.

It's a common thought among job seekers that former employers can't or won't divulge damning information about you. And to an extent they are correct. The smart professional knows that reference information can be used or misused and they could find themselves in the hot seat for giving a bad (or sometimes good) reference. But this is not failsafe protection from negative reports on your behavior. Remember: The hiring world is a world of relationships. And people know people. And people talk to people - about other people. And they say it's "off the record" which in some twisted way protects them from slander or libel suits. So protect yourself. Learn who's going to say what about you before you give an unconditional OK to "check my references."

An MPC Is Willing To Work In A Cooperative Vein

In my world of being a recruiter, the more cooperative a candidate was, the more likely I was to expend my effort to get him or her placed. The more cooperative an employer was, the more likely I was to expend my effort to find the very best candidates for the company. It's the golden rule, right? Better yet, it's just good karma. If you want to land a job in a crummy economy - or in any economy for that matter! - ya gotta do whatever it takes to get the job done.

Let me give you an example of a situation that I've encountered many times that will demonstrate what a lack of cooperation looks like. It has to do with the application form. A candidate would arrive at my office and would be given several forms to fill out by our receptionist. I can think of a few instances when our receptionist would come back to my desk, empty paperwork in hand and say, "She won't fill this out until she can talk to you." Some candidates would refuse - yes, I said refuse - to fill out the application before they would speak with a recruiter. Now, I'm sure there were many reasons that these people were motivated to not comply/cooperate, but I'm sure none of them had anything to do with the receptionist or with me. Quite likely, they had had a negative experience at another recruiting company, and they wanted to make sure that history did not repeat itself. Unfortunately, though, by not cooperating, they ensured that history would indeed repeat itself, because what self-respecting recruiter wants to spend much time assisting a candidate who has made a negative judgment before attempting to develop a good working relationship? Cooperation goes a long way. It's not wrong to have questions, and it's not wrong to ask them. It is, however, advisable to let questions be posed in a positive and constructive way, so they will not make you look uncooperative or, worse yet, distrustful.

So Are You An MPC?

If you are, then it's time to market this product called "You." But if you aren't experienced in this idea of marketing, you might not know where to begin. In my experience, the answer to the question, "Where do I start?" is closer than you think.

putting

yourself
under the *microscope*

Chapter 6

How many of us think we really know who we are and what makes us tick? Further, how many of us think this is really important when searching for a job? I have found that the more you know about you, the more likely you are to land in a position... and to land in one that is satisfying.

6

Start With You

Do you remember the first thing professional recruiters do? They establish what the product is.

How much do you know about you?

When is the last time you sat down and really put yourself under the microscope?

I'm not talking about what you like to do or what you think you are good at. I'm talking about who you are at the core.

Unless you understand what makes you tick, you will be at a disadvantage when you take you - the product - to the marketplace. You will run the risk of accepting a job that is not right for you.

To demonstrate my point, I am going to use a "non-human" example. Let's say you are planning to buy a car. You have to know about the car's features. You have to be able to describe:

What type of vehicle you want to buy

How much it costs or how much you can afford

What it looks like

How fast it goes

How safe it is

What kind of gas mileage it gets

What its resale potential is

...and the list goes on.

Each feature you explore about this vehicle helps you develop a picture of the ideal car you'll potentially purchase. But next you have to ask a different level of question to understand what will make you buy one car vs. another. And that question is, **"What's Important?"** Of all the features that you have described and explored, which rise to the top?

Is it the look and feel?

Is it the safety rating?

Is it the resale potential?

What's important?

These features translate into benefits you will experience after making the purchase. When you find a model that is pleasing to the eye, you may feel more attractive behind the wheel; if the car has high safety ratings, you benefit by feeling secure every time you drive your children to school. You'll buy the car because of the benefits you'll receive just as you'll accept a position because of the benefits you'll receive.

So, when you are in a job search, the answers to the question "What's Important?" are at the core of landing the job of your dreams. The answers to these questions are your core values. For instance, if job security is important, when you find a job opportunity working for a company that has had a stable history, you benefit by knowing that each day you drive into the office, there is a job waiting for you.

Just like buying a car, you are buying a job. Not just for its features, but because it provides you with what's important to "You." It provides you with a way to live in congruence with your values. It allows you to do what you are vs. doing merely what you are good at. And yes, it is possible. I am living proof.

In 2004, when I made the decision to embark upon a career in coaching, many of my colleagues voiced their concern. Why would I move away from doing something I was so good at? I had worked for 14 years as a recruiter, and I was *really* good at it. I had a solid clientele of companies that relied on me to find the very best person to support their top level executive, and I attracted amazingly talented executive assistants who relied upon me to help them make smooth career transitions. Why in the world would I want to "ruin a good thing?" Because I wasn't doing "what I was." I was doing "what I was good at."

In the couple of years leading up to 2004, I had begun to explore what was important to me. And I discovered that my job as a recruiter wasn't totally in line with what was important to me.

Here's what emerged when I explored what my core values are vs. what my job was:

Core Value

Quality Relationships

Because the job of a recruiter is more transactional than relational (and I'm not saying I didn't develop some great relationships as a recruiter), I felt a disconnect. Sometimes, to get the result (a placement), I would have to put the relationship in the background.

Integrity, Trust And Open Communications

Again, to get the result (the placement) recruiters at times finds themselves in the position of not giving full information - almost lying by omission.

Ongoing Personal Development

Having done the recruiting job successfully for so many years, my own personal development had been put on the back burner. I'd "been there/done that," and while I would say "there's always something to learn," in my job of recruiter, there was not much more for me in the personal/professional growth area.

Creativity

Having been in the recruiting field so long, I had become a machine carrying out the task of conducting searches effectively, and since the results were good, I found little reason to use much creativity.

Inner Harmony

A successful recruiter's mindset includes self talk that sounds something like this: "OK, I closed the placement, now let's hope it works." There are so many variables that can get in the way of a successful hire, and those variables are so far outside the control of the recruiter, the last thing a closed placement generates is a sense of inner harmony.

Helping Others Reach Their Greatest Potential

While my recruiting efforts indeed helped my candidates move forward in their careers, I didn't always feel as if I was helping them reach their "greatest" potential.

Abundance

I must admit this core value was fulfilled in the practice of recruiting. The income potential of many other professions pales in comparison to the revenues generated by a successful recruiter.

> I wasn't doing "what I was."
> I was doing "what I was good at."

When I put the pencil to the paper and wrote down what was most important to me at the very core, I realized that while I was doing what I was good at, I was not living true to my core values.

Developing Your Life Vision

To develop your life vision, you have to start with who you are at the very core. And that means taking a look at your core values. The things that make you tick. Not what you do, or what you want to do, but who you are. Steven Covey put it well when he said, "How different our lives are when we really know what is deeply important to us, and, keeping that picture in mind, we manage ourselves each day to be and to know what really matters most."

When you identify your **core values**, you're in a much *better* position to develop the **Life Vision** that will guide you toward that *ideal job* or career.

So how do you do it?

On the next page is an exercise you can do that will help you identify your core values so you can develop your Life Vision.

Core Values Sample List

Abundance

Acceptance

Achievement

Advancement

Adventure

Affection (love and caring)

Appearance

Authenticity

Authority

Beauty/good looks

Being around like-minded people

Belonging/feeling connected

Career

Challenge

Change and variety

Charity

Communication

Community

Community service

Compassion

Competence

Competition

Cooperation

Courage

Creativity

Decisiveness

Democracy

Diplomacy

Effective communications

Effectiveness

Efficiency

Environment

Excellence

Excitement

Expertise

Fairness

Faith

Fame

Family

Fast living

Fast-paced work

Fidelity

Financial gain

Financial security

Forgiveness

Freedom

Friendship

Growth

Happiness

Having a family

Health

Healthy relationships

Helping

Honesty

Independence

Influence

Influencing others

Inner harmony

Integrity

Intellectual status

Intimacy

Involvement

Joy

Continued on next page. . .

Justice
Knowledge
Leadership ✳
Love
Loyalty
Meaningful work
Merit
Money
Neatness ✳
Order (tranquility, stability)
Others
Peace
Perseverance
Persistence
Personal growth ✳
Physical challenge
Pleasure
Power
Privacy
Professional development
Promotional opportunities
Prosperity
Public service
Quality relationships
Rationality
Recognition
Reputation
Respect from others
Responsibility and accountability
Security
Self-Acceptance, self-respect
Self-control
Serenity
Service to others

Spiritual growth
Spirituality
Stability
Status
Success ✳
Teamwork
Time freedom
Tolerance
Tradition
Trust
Truth
Wealth ✳
Wisdom

_____

_____

_____

_____

Determining Your Core Values

1 Read through the list of values. Some will be important to you; some might not be. Go though the list, and this first time, **circle any and all of the values that are true for you.** Add any to the bottom that you don't see listed that you feel are important to you.

You'll notice there are many words on this list that have NOTHING to do with a job or finding a job. Why? Your values and your Life Vision are way bigger than a job. They are way bigger than your career. They are a reflection of you, the person. Not just you the employee.

Digression For Skeptics

Is This Really Important?

I know there are skeptics out there right now reading this who are saying, "Does this really matter? What does creating my vision have anything to do with finding a job?" Well, I'm going to ask you to step out of your job-seeking shoes for just a minute to demonstrate this point.

Have you ever planned a party? Any kind of party. Whether it was a good party or not doesn't matter. Whether people had a good time or not doesn't matter. Just think of a party that you had control of putting together. First, you had to decide that whatever occasion it was celebrating was worthy of you exerting effort on planning, right? Next, you probably had to consider what day to have it on, where to have it, who to invite, what to serve, etc. You may have spent a lot of time on the details or maybe no time whatsoever. The party may have been a huge success or it might have been a total disaster. In any event, that party began with a vision. And every part of that planning process began with a value of some kind. Every action became an expression of what's important. Still unclear?

Action	Value
Have a party	Being around lots of people
Have party on Sunday	Family time/quality relationships
Host/Plan the party	Leadership
Create a guest list	Maintaining friendships
Celebrate a graduation	Encouraging education/achievement
Choose the venue	Beauty/aesthetically pleasing surroundings

Here's a professional example: If you are a carpenter, you aren't just a carpenter because you are good with a hammer. There's something much bigger than that at work. Maybe you are a carpenter whose vision is creating beauty with a natural medium while contributing to the community by helping to develop the talents of others. You still use a hammer, but you're doing so for a much bigger reason.

Your Life Vision is much **bigger** than what you are *good* at or what you do.

It's much **bigger** than your career.

It's **who you are** as a person and what is *important* to you.

2 Go back through the items you circled and **narrow your list to ten**. Which items are more important to you than the others? **Place a star** next to your top ten values.

3 **Now imagine this:** You are at the end of your life. You are visited by the person who will deliver your eulogy. He has one request. He asks you, "Of the ten values you feel have guided you through your life, which three do you feel are the most important?" You have to choose. Which will you throw away from your list of ten? What will remain? **Circle these three values.**

Writing Your Life Vision

Now you are ready to develop your Life Vision based upon your core values. When you write your vision, you must include the top three, but you may also wish to dip into the top ten.

Here are a couple examples:

Success • Career • Balance

"My life vision is a world where I balance a successful career and a happy home life. This vision includes me leading a successful business and sharing my experience and knowledge with others."

Quality Relationships • Communications • Development

"My life vision is a vision of all people having quality relationships based upon integrity and open communications. It's a world that values ongoing professional and personal development and creativity and recognizes that true success comes from helping others reach their greatest potential."

Once you understand what your Life Vision is, you are ready to move toward the next step in understanding your MPC. Your product. Yourself.

What Are Your Strengths And Weaknesses?

How many of us truly know what our strengths and weaknesses are? For many years, I thought I knew what mine were, but right around the time I turned 40, I realized I didn't have a clue about my strengths. Ever hear the phrase, "You don't know what you don't know?" Well, I didn't know what I didn't know. All this time I thought I knew what I was good at, but it took a few years of self examination and assessment to really understand what my true gifts - and corresponding weaknesses! - looked like.

But how do you figure that out more quickly? If you're in a career search, you don't have the luxury of time. Earlier, I mentioned the SWOT analysis. Take the time to understand your strengths, your weaknesses, the potential opportunities for success and possible threats to your achieving success. This is a great exercise to explore who you are from a rational and conscious perspective.

I would also recommend getting a picture of "the real you" by taking some assessments that give you insight from a few different perspectives.

Here are some suggestions:

Types Of Assessments

Before I enter a discussion about assessments, I'd like to answer a question that you may be asking: "Why should I spend money on assessments?" This is a valid question, especially if you are currently unemployed. But, while your inclination is to look at the immediate picture (i.e. I need a job!), I am suggesting that you look at the bigger, more long-range picture. This picture includes not just what you "can" do, but what you are really meant to do. And the only way to discover what you are meant to do is to explore how you are wired. Am I saying that once you understand what you are meant to do, you will automatically land that type of job? Maybe you will; maybe you won't. But in my life as a coach, I have seen people reach goals that at the outset seemed insurmountable just because they did one thing: they considered what was possible.

Again, it goes back to the Law of Attraction. If you can create a picture of what you are great at or what you would naturally excel at, you are much more likely to attract opportunities that are in harmony with that image. Assessments are the tools a person uses to explore the product called "You" in a way that can't be done by simply doing a self-inventory.

Why?

Because while most of us have a sense for who we are (after all, we are living inside our own skin), we lack the necessary objectivity to really understand how we are wired. Assessments give you perspective from the outside in. As you begin to explore the inner workings of you - the behavior the world sees, the way you naturally process information, how you learn, how you handle conflict or what your preferences are – you will start to get a clearer picture of the types of positions that will complement your style.

DiSC®

This assessment is used by many career, business and life coaches because it identifies behaviors that are observable and predictable. It shows the person being assessed how his behavior impacts his environment and how the environment impacts his behavior. This assessment is administered online, and is most valuable if the person being assessed is debriefed by someone knowledgeable about the DiSC® tool.

MBTI – Myers Briggs

This assessment is widely used by people in the human resources and consulting industries. The essence of MBTI theory is that a lot of what seems to be random variation in a person's behavior is actually orderly and consistent, due to basic differences in how a person prefers to use his or her perception and judgment.

Strengthsfinder®

This tool, developed by the Gallup Organization, is used by many corporations for the purpose of employee development. Strengthsfinder® promotes the idea that we are all predisposed to 5 top strengths that seem to guide our actions. This assessment is self-administered, online. One must only purchase the book *Now, Discover Your Strengths*, by Marcus Buckingham, to obtain the online code for the assessment.

There are countless other assessments you can take.

There are assessments that describe how you learn (Kolb), how you react to conflict (Thomas Kilman, Inc. Conflict Model), how you notice things (Enneagram), what your general preferences are (Reiss)... the list goes on.

For the sake of simplicity, I would recommend you take one (or maybe two) assessments. After all, your time and resources are limited, and your goal is to get a new job - not to get too bogged down in the analysis. Believe me, it's easy to do. This stuff can be eye opening and become really distracting if you let it. The assessments I described above (DiSC®, MBTI, and Strengthsfinder®) are all relatively inexpensive, easily understood, and applicable to the task of career search. Once you have completed the assessment phase, you should be getting a clearer picture of how your strengths fit within your Overall Life Vision.

If after completing some assessments (or if you are dead set against doing some assessment work) you are still unclear about what your strengths are, I would recommend asking people. Talk to your former bosses, coworkers, subordinates. Ask them what they feel your greatest strengths are. This is also a great way to hear what these folks will most likely say when they receive a call checking your references.

If you're still unclear about what your strengths are after these exercises, pull out your old performance appraisals. Surely, you will find some clues about what the world sees as your strengths. In any event, don't just rely on what *you* feel your strengths are.

YOU *are* inside your skin *looking out. . .*

...the *world* is seeing you through a different lens.

Why is it important to know who you are?

My understanding of myself and my ability to articulate it paid great dividends for me.

I'll give you an example that happened in my early career as a coach. A large company was considering me for a contract position coaching several teams of employees. It was a project that I estimated could result in revenues of around $50-75K over a six-month period. As I sat in the lobby, I anxiously wondered what I could possibly present to the President of this company that would make me stand out from the other coaches who were under consideration. I didn't have any flashy PowerPoint presentation. No bar graphs or charts with HR metrics that would indicate that I had a clue about the best way to motivate people or build teams. And then the realization came to me. They needed to know ME in order to make a decision. They weren't hiring a program. They were hiring a person. My prediction was accurate. The first question they asked me was, "Tell me about yourself."

Fortunately, I had jotted down the results of the many assessments I had taken over the course of the last year, and I began to explain to them not just what my experience or history was, but who I really was. I was able to paint a picture of what my strengths were and what my weaknesses were. I shared with them what my behavior looked like, what my preferences were, how I processed information, how I gave information and a host of other tendencies that I felt would give them a true picture of me.

I left the interview feeling I had gotten my point across but wondering if I had taken the right approach. Two weeks later, I was brought in again and asked to begin working with their teams. *I got* the job! I asked the President what had caused him to hire me over the other coaches he was considering. His answer? "Because I like *who* you are. And I believe *who* you are and how you operate is a fit for my people." My understanding of myself and my ability to articulate it, had paid great dividends for me.

exploring your current reality

Chapter 7

To land a job you must have
a good understanding of your
current reality. When you think
of the jobs you have had,
what worked? What didn't?
So often, when we are looking
for a job – especially in a crummy
economy – we think only of what
we CAN do and we fail to
consider what we really
WANT to do.

7

So you've taken stock of what you are good at. What your strengths are. What your limitations are. But what are your likes? What are your preferences? I had lunch with a development officer of a major university who shared a story with me about her assistant. This development officer was new to her role, and her assistant had been employed by the university for a few years prior. It was pretty obvious that the assistant was unhappy, and the development officer was very certain she was in the midst of looking for a new job. Rather than simply let this person go, the development officer sat down with the assistant, let her know that she noticed her displeasure with her current situation, and then asked this question: "What would you like to do?" The assistant, with tears in her eyes, replied, "No one has ever asked me that question." Hundreds of job seekers have expressed the same thing to me when we meet to discuss their ideal next position. "No one has ever asked me what it is I 'want' to do. Rather, I am only asked what it is I 'can' do." Knowing an employer won't always ask this question of you, it then becomes your responsibility to ask yourself the question BEFORE embarking on a career search.

What is it you *really* like to do?

Here are some brainstorming questions. Write down as many ideas as come to mind, and then go back to see what patterns might emerge.

In each job I have had (or if you have been with one employer for a long time, in each assignment you have had) what were the tasks or responsibilities I enjoyed the very most?

———————————————————————————

———————————————————————————

———————————————————————————

———————————————————————————

Which job or assignment did I enjoy the most? What was it about this job or assignment that really excited me?

_____

_____

_____

_____

What tasks do I look forward to accomplishing? What things do I tend to do first?

_____

_____

_____

_____

What projects have I been involved in that I really enjoyed?

_____

_____

_____

_____

What skills have I used that really excited me?

Organizing / planning

What do I prefer to do at work?

Now look at each job or assignment from the opposing viewpoint. You need to explore the areas that are turnoffs or things you would want to avoid.

In each job I have had (or if you have been with one employer for a long time, in each assignment you have had) what were the tasks or responsibilities I enjoyed the very least?

Which job or assignment did I enjoy the least? What was it about this job or assignment that really turned me off?

_____

_____

_____

_____

What tasks do I dread accomplishing? What things do I tend to put off until last?

_____

_____

_____

_____

What projects have I been involved in that I really did NOT enjoy?

_____

_____

_____

_____

What skills have I used that I don't care to use?

_____

_____

_____

_____

Chapter 8

Many job seekers embark on a
career search without clearly
defining their vision for their next
position. These people believe
that the best way to get back to
work is to immediately get busy.
I agree that you need to get busy,
but first, you need to get busy
designing your next position.

How Would You Define Your Ideal Next Position?

You may say, "There's no such thing as an ideal position," or "If there's an ideal position out there, I'll be surprised." But I say, "If you don't have a target, your search will be just as good as arriving at a vacation destination without a map." If you don't know where you're going, while you're sure to get *somewhere*, you're not quite sure if somewhere is the place you'd really like to be. Over the years, I've seen thousands of people engaged in job searches. And the majority of them conduct these searches without a clear vision of what their ultimate target is. So in the next few pages, you are going to design a template for three possible scenarios: your ideal job, your next job and any job.

Why develop a template? As you go through the many activities involved in conducting an effective career search, you will be faced with the task of comparing many different options. If you do not have a target, or a template against which to compare all of your options, you will have difficulty in making a sound decision.

Let's use the analogy of an archer who is perfecting his aim. He puts a target off in the distance, and shoots at it from the same spot over and over again. After each shot, he adjusts his stance or his aim until he finally hits the bull's eye. If he did not have a target to shoot at and if he did not return to the same vantage point to shoot, he would be less likely to hit the bull's eye.

Similarly, you the job seeker need a target if you want to conduct a successful search. You need something to shoot for: the ideal position. Then after each interview you go on, you can compare that opportunity with the ideal target you have developed. You'll look at the opportunity, adjust your strategy and move closer to the ideal position.

Designing The Ideal Job

First, let's look at the ideal job. The ideal job is the place you see yourself ending up. It's a true reflection of you and your core values. The ideal job is one that pays the salary or wage you would like to earn, and involves doing all the things you like to do. It truly utilizes all your talents and offers you the many long-range opportunities that are important to you. You have already begun to define the ideal job by exploring your core values, assessing your current reality, and completing your personal SWOT analysis.

What's important to me?

Title - I always ask people to open their minds to titles they might not normally be attracted to when they design their ideal job. In my world of executive assistant placements, the word "secretary" holds a negative connotation for some, but to avoid a job simply because of its title could cause you to bypass a great career opportunity just because the company's HR representative hasn't stayed up with the times and updated titles. Look beyond the title, but recognize (based upon your strengths and weaknesses and what you like and don't like) what existing titles feel like a fit to you.

For example, if you are a marketing professional, your title might be marketing coordinator, or project manager, or marketing administrator, or new business development associate, or inside sales representative, or sales manager - to name a few. Remember: What you call yourself or what your company calls you is just a label. And every other company uses labels that may or may not be similar.

In my recruiting world, I place the assistant to the top-level executive of an organization. She (or he) may be given one of many titles.

For instance:

Executive Secretary

Secretary

Administrative Assistant

Executive Administrative Assistant

Administrative Secretary

Office Administrator

Assistant

Personal Executive Assistant

Executive Coordinator

Assistant to the _____ (fill in the blank)

Senior Administrative Assistant

Administrative Services Coordinator

Executive Office Assistant

Assistant to the Executive Office

So as you are defining your ideal job, explore the position's responsibilities, the level of authority, the reporting relationships, the goals of the position, etc. to decide if it's right for you - and if you're right for the job. But list all of the titles that would be acceptable to you as you define the ideal job.

Brainstorming Exercise: Titles

What are you going to do in your next job? What are those jobs called?
What are the titles? What are the responsibilities?

Job Titles   Job Responsibilities

_____   _____

_____   _____

_____   _____

_____   _____

_____   _____

_____   _____

Do a little research. If you haven't held a wide variety of jobs, but you would like to branch out, go online and start reading job descriptions that are similar to what you have done or what you would like to do. What titles are associated with these positions?

Does it really matter what you are called? Maybe it does or maybe it doesn't. Either way, you need to know what the industry is calling people who do what you do in the environments within which you would like to work.

Location – Where Do You Want Your Job To Be Located?

To give you a context on location: I built my recruiting business in a suburb of Detroit. In this area (the motor city!), professionals rely on automobiles to get them to and from work everyday. Unfortunately, our region hasn't yet developed a transit system that is used by the masses. Typically, here in the metro area, a commuting professional can expect to drive 30-45 minutes one way to work. Most folks don't relish the idea of being in their car for more than an hour and a half per day, and companies are hesitant to hire people who will have to drive much longer either. Their feelings are that as soon as an opportunity closer presents itself, the employee will make the move for convenience's sake. Right or wrong, it's a common perception. So keep your sights on jobs within a reasonable commuting range of your home.

But what if there aren't opportunities within this range? Some regions (and I happen to live and work in one of them) are losing people due to the challenging economic climate. In 2007, Michigan was one of only two states in the US that lost people (we lost more than five times the national average, in fact!). So, if you find yourself living in a region where opportunities just don't exist in your line of work, it may be time to start the process of relocation. Better yet, it may be time to start the process of reinvention. But that's a subject for another book.

Brainstorming Exercise:

What locations would you consider for the ideal job:

Location	Benefits	Obstacles

Salary - How Much Is Enough?

Just as you need to define the titles that will be acceptable to you in your ideal job, you need to determine what salary you will accept. I will tell you what I have seen in the last 20 years related to STARTING salaries. An employed person who accepts a similar position within a similar company can expect to receive an offer anywhere from at LEAST the amount he or she is currently earning to at MOST ten percent more. This is also assuming that other factors are the same (benefits, etc.). Are there exceptions? Yes. But again, what I have seen is that employers don't normally offer people more than a 10% raise simply for showing up to an interview and extolling their virtues. Employers want to see what you can do rather than simply hear about it from you.

Consider also potential earnings that come from bonuses, overtime, profit sharing, etc. Are there built-in earnings beyond the salary? What about performance reviews? What is the potential to earn more? How often are you evaluated and upon what criteria is your performance judged?

Salary Brainstorm:

What salary did I earn in my last job?

How long was I at that salary level?

How does my salary compare with people doing the same work in a different company?

How does my salary compare to salaries in other geographic regions?

How was my salary structured? Was I paid hourly? Did I receive overtime? Did I receive bonuses?

What would the ideal salary structure look like for me?

Benefits Exploration:

Part of an employee's compensation is fringe benefits. And benefits can vary greatly from firm to firm and industry to industry. The best place to start when determining what benefits are important is to focus on where you are right now. Ask yourself: what benefits do I currently have that I will need in my next position? And then, what benefits do I NOT currently enjoy that I would like to see in my next position? Here are some things to consider:

Type of Benefit	Current Reality: What do I currently have?	Desired Reality: What do I wish I had?	Level of Importance: How important is this to me right now?
Healthcare			
Dependent Coverage			
Dental			
Optical			
Tuition Assistance			
Life Insurance			
Short Term Disability			
Long Term Disability			
Pension			
Profit Sharing			
401(k)/Savings Plan			
Vacation Time			
Sick Time			
Personal Time			
Expense Allowance			
Other Benefits			
Other Benefits			

Healthcare

Healthcare coverage is a hot topic for job seekers. Take a moment to consider what's important to you when it comes to healthcare. Begin by reviewing your current reality and expand to what you will expect in your next positions. Here are some questions to consider:

Who is my insurance carrier?

Do I need to retain this carrier? (For instance, do I have a pre-existing medical condition that would require me to have the same type of insurance?)

What health coverage do I have now that I will need? (Do I have dental, optical, prescription, etc.?)

Do I cover my dependents? Do I need to cover my dependents?

How much do I pay for my benefits (consider premiums, co-pays, deductibles)?

When I am hired, how soon do I become eligible for healthcare and other benefits? (Will there be a lapse in coverage?)

How much will I pay to retain my coverage (to avoid a lapse in coverage)?

Putting It All Together: My Ideal Position

What are the titles I will ideally hold?	
What industries am I most interested in and marketable within?	
What are the locations I desire to work within?	
What realistic salary is most acceptable to me?	
What benefits do I currently enjoy that I will need?	
What are the ideal hours I will work?	
What's my #1 Priority in my next job?	
What's my #2 Priority in my next job?	

But What If The Ideal Position Is Just Not Available?

I am writing these words in 2009 - one of the most challenging times in the world of employment, especially in the Detroit marketplace. It is entirely possible that the ideal position that you have described is difficult or seemingly impossible to find. What do you do in this instance? Do you throw up your hands and resign yourself to a life of unemployment? Or do you consider other possibilities?

If you are looking for a job in a "Crummy Economy," defining the ideal job may not be enough. During times of high unemployment, it is very likely that a person will not land immediately in the ideal job. So, what job can you look for in this case?

Designing The Next Job

This is the job that can move you toward the ideal job. People who are looking for the next job understand that it is likely that the ideal job may not exist at the moment. But these people also know that they need to earn income to meet their basic needs. However, they would prefer not to land in just *any* job, because it might not lead them to the ideal job. Their preference is to land a job that is a stepping stone to the ideal job. Here are some examples:

I'm a laid-off factory worker whose ideal job is to work in customer service or sales. Ideally, I'll work in an office handling customer inquiries, etc. But realistically, I need to get some experience dealing with the public. I need to earn some money (*any* job) but I want to get to customer service or sales (*ideal* job) so I might take a job working in a retail store or in the restaurant or hospitality industry (*next* job) to get some exposure to handling the people side of things. Make sense?

I'm a laid-off secretary who worked in a corporate office of an automotive supplier. My salary was pretty high when I was laid off, so I'm not sure I'll get a job at this level (*ideal* job) right away. I do know I need to pay my mortgage so I need a job (*any* job), but I would like to work in an environment where people like my former boss frequent. Back in college, I worked as a waitress, so maybe I can get a waitress job at an upscale breakfast restaurant or dinner venue (*next* job.) And just maybe, I'll connect with my potential next boss or someone who is impressed enough with me that they connect me with my potential next boss.

The next job may not be doing exactly what you plan to do in the ideal job, but it will either prepare you for it by building your skills in a particular area, or it will put you in contact with the people who need to know you in order to consider you for your ideal job.

The Next Job: What Does It Look Like For You?

What titles could lead me to the ideal job?	
What industries are related to my ideal industry?	
What locations will I consider?	
What salary will I accept?	
What benefits will I accept?	
What hours am I available to work?	
What's my #1 Priority in my next job?	
What's my #2 Priority in my next job?	

What are the differences between the ideal job and the next job for you?

How do you feel about the next job? Do you feel like you are settling? Or do you feel like you are taking a step forward?

What mental adjustments will you need to make to get excited about landing in the next job?

Defining Any Job

But what if your unemployment benefits have run out? What if you are not in a financial position to wait for that ideal job?

Maybe it will be necessary for you to take the third category of job: any job.

The person who says he needs any job just needs to make enough money to pay the bills. If you fall into this category then you'll most likely have to be satisfied with making less than what you'd really like to make, and you'll probably be doing something other than what you want to be doing - but you will be earning cash to take care of your basic needs.

It's not a bad thing to look for any job. In fact, in today's economy, many people displaced by the automotive crisis find themselves in this position. But, just be conscious of what you are doing. Be aware that right now, you are looking for a means to an end. And that end is to pay the bills.

Defining Any Job: What Does Any Job Look Like For You?

What are all the titles I am prepared to consider?	
What are all the industries I will work within?	
What are all the locations I will consider?	
What is the minimum salary I can accept?	
What benefits must I have?	
What hours will I work?	

Self-Reflection Questions

What sorts of things emerged as you defined the ideal job vs. the next job vs. any job?

What adjustments might you need to make as you move forward toward each of these types of jobs?

How long are you prepared to hold *any* job?

Can you continue to look for a new position while you work in *any* job?

where to market yourself

Chapter 9

Every marketing professional
knows in order to successfully
sell a product, he needs to
know the customer. When you
are looking for a job (selling your
MPC), you need to know about
your customer (the person
who is going to hire you).
Knowing where to market
yourself will require you to do
a little homework on who will
be most attracted to you.

So, What's Next?

We've spent a lot of time on who the product is – you. What you're good at, what you're not so good at, what you want and what you don't want. You have developed a template called the Ideal Position. Now you need to figure out where to find that position. That's what the professional recruiter does after she has identified her MPC. Here are some of the considerations you, the recruiter, will need to make as you move forward:

Where Do You Market Your MPC: What Industry?

I remember one of my trainers explaining the importance of selecting the proper market for my MPC. She would say "Taking your MPC to the wrong market (industry) is as effective as selling refrigerators in Amish country."

You have to present your product "You" to companies who are in a position to use your industry experience. Why? At a fundamental level, employers wonder "can he or she do the job?" as they are considering someone for a position. If you have worked in a similar environment or industry, the employer's logical conclusion is that you will "fit in" on even the most basic level. After this initial determination of fit between you and their environment, the employer will consider how long it will take to get you up and running. Learning curves, a combination of hiring costs and assimilation expenses, add up in a hurry! How long will it be before you are productive or revenue-producing? Again, at a basic level, the employer's assumption is "if he's done the job for a similar company, he'll most likely be able to learn our system quickly and cost-effectively."

So the question the job seeker must answer is: What industry will benefit the most from hiring me? The obvious answer is: The industry within which you last worked. The not-so-obvious answer is: The industry within which you worked prior to your last job. Reach back to other jobs you have held in other companies and other industries.

As an example, when I became a recruiter, one of the advantages I felt I had over other recruiters who had worked for only one or two companies was that over the years, I had been employed within a diverse array of industries. In fact, most people would have looked at my work history as lacking stability, but I saw it as preparing me to adapt to many different industries or cultures. Between the years 1980 and 1989, I worked for:

A gubernatorial campaign office (government)

A grocery store (food industry)

A department store (retail industry)

An automotive manufacturer (manufacturing or automotive industry)

A telephone company (utility)

A property/casualty insurance company (insurance industry)

A temporary services company (staffing industry)

A college bookstore (educational institution)

A bank (banking industry)

Because I had exposure to all these industries I could "talk the talk," so to speak, at a meeting with hiring managers, and more often than not they would hire me *because I understood the uniqueness of their industry or culture.*

So look at all the places you have worked.

List all the types of environments within which you have worked:

Company	Industry Or Environment

If you worked for only one company, look at the various departments or divisions you worked for. For instance, if you worked for 15 years at a manufacturing company, but worked within operations for 5 years, sales for 2 years and purchasing for the remaining years, list each of these items separately.

What was it about the various settings that you liked? Which environments did you feel you fit best within? Why? Take a moment to brainstorm and come up with all the possible types of companies that you would both like to work within and companies that would be attracted to your experience.

Industry Or Environment	How It Fits With You

What Locations?

Where do you want to work from
a geographic perspective?

Is relocation a possibility?

Where are the jobs you're most
interested in located?

In my world, I see most people wishing to stay in Southeastern Michigan. It's an interesting phenomenon, but we Michiganders love our state, and most of us just don't want to leave. Come on... we have hundreds of lakes, beautiful shorelines, four gorgeous seasons and people who are simply the salt of the earth! Even if our state is in an economic crisis, people who are born here tend to want to stay here.

Just as an example: Of the nearly 30,000 living alumni from my alma mater, Wayne State University School of Business (located in the heart of Detroit), 20,000 live in Michigan still. And 80% of those folks still live in Southeastern Michigan. And I've read billboards from other major Michigan universities that boast the same retention rate.

So when I am interviewing an individual who lives and works in the metro area, I explain to them that the commuting professional wants to work within 30-45 minutes of home. This is pretty consistent across metropolitan areas. People do not wish to spend more than 15-20% of their time during the week stuck in traffic. And employers shy away from employees whose commute is longer than an hour, one way, from home. Let's be practical. What's going to happen if there is a snowstorm (which happens in Michigan) or if there is a traffic emergency (which happens in all American cities)? Employers are sensitive to the possibility that an employee who lives far away will be absent from work if their commute is longer than average. I remember placing an executive secretary who lived in Rochester (a suburb north of Detroit) into a position supporting a CEO whose office was in Taylor (a suburb south of Detroit.) Her daily commute was just over 48 miles… or, as we say in Michigan, she worked about an hour and fifteen minutes from home on a good day. Because of the level of her position, missing work was not an option. So in the event of a snowstorm, she stayed at a hotel near work, and always kept an overnight bag at the office for just this type of emergency.

What are your feelings on commuting? Can you imagine yourself in this sort of situation? If not, keep your search to businesses located within a 45 minute commute of your home.

What Companies?

When I interview candidates, I typically will ask for the names of companies for which they would like to work. **Develop a list of companies you would like to work for AND a list of companies you would NOT like to work for**. Be sure to identify companies that would be most attracted to someone with your skills and experience too. Here are some questions you can use to brainstorm in developing such a list:

Who would be most attracted to someone like me?

A company that sells a consumer product will be attracted to someone who has experience working within a company that sells another consumer product.

An organization dedicated to a certain cause will likely be attracted to a person who has experience working within a not-for-profit setting.

Service-based industries (healthcare, insurance, etc.) look often for individuals who have worked for other service-based companies.

Companies that actually manufacture a product look to hire candidates coming from organizations that employ manufacturing processes to make their money.

So open your mind to how the employer will view you from this perspective. Start from their vantage point. Imagine you are a healthcare organization. Who might you be most attracted to, based solely upon their industry experience? Not sure? Tap into your network. Talk to people who come from the healthcare industry and ask them. If their jobs don't give them the information that you need, ask them who they know within their organizations who might be able to give you this information. Remember: You are involved in the process of searching for a job... it's a process. With each interaction, you are moving closer to your target.

What Organizations Would I Be Most Attracted To?

Earlier, we talked about the types of positions that you would be attracted to. Let's now take a broader, more macro look at the types of organizations or industries within which you would like to work. The obvious answer to this question is to target companies engaged in a business similar to your current employer. Perhaps approach competitors of your current employer. But what if you are up for a change? Where do you start to set your sights outside of your current industry?

Here are some points of exploration:

Companies that offer what is important to you (Remember our discussion on what is important to you?)

Highest paying companies (Perhaps pay is very high on
your list of priorities. How do you find out who the highest
paying companies are?)

Best and brightest to work for?

Every region has an organization that publishes lists of the "best companies" to
work for. And they are deemed the "best" based upon a broad range of criteria.
In Southeastern Michigan, we have the "101 Best and Brightest Companies to Work
For" published by the Michigan Business & Professional Association, a business
organization that represents companies that employ over 120,000 persons throughout
the State of Michigan. On a national level, you'll find lists like Fortune Magazine's 100
Best Companies for Women to Work For. Or maybe you want to work for one of the
fastest growth companies as listed by the Wall Street Journal. The lists are out there,
so choose your favorite search engine, type in the parameters that are important to
you, and **generate a target list to begin your search.**

Target List

_____

_____

_____

_____

_____

_____

_____

So now you have the list of the companies you'd like to target. But what next?

You're going to need to find out a little more about these companies. You're going to need to explore what's important to these companies. But where do you begin? You're probably sitting near the very place you'll find the data that will carry you to next step. Whether you're using a laptop, a Blackberry or a desktop, get online and start the exploration. This is one of the fun parts of finding that ideal job. This is the time when you open up your eyes to possibilities you might not have considered before. This is the time you can find out lots about companies without being under scrutiny yourself. You'll be in the privacy of your own home - or maybe you'll be in the library if you don't have your own computer hook up - but in any event, you will be in a position to do some behind-the-scenes investigation into your next possible employer. Make this fun. Make it interesting.

Still not sure where to start?

Start with the company's own web site. What is its overall look and feel? Progressive? Traditional? High-tech? People-friendly? Product-driven? How easy is it to navigate around? Can you start to understand the company's culture or its priorities? What do its leaders look like? Do you see diversity? Look at their career section. Are there lots of jobs listed? Does it look like they are expanding? Read the job descriptions and requirements. What types of people do they look for? What types of skills and background? Do their priorities seem to be in line with your experience in a general sense? The company's web site will give you a very good view from *the company's* perspective.

But what do other people have to say about the company?

How do you figure this out?

The easiest way to find out more information is to type in the company name into a search engine and see what comes up. What articles have been written about the company? Type in the names of the company's leaders. What articles have been written about those people? There are volumes of information about companies on the web if you open your mind and explore the possibilities. The information you gather will begin to give you a picture of what makes that company tick and what is important to them. Given this information, you can then decide if the company, its values, etc. are in line with your Life Vision; if so, you can move forward.

So now you have a list of companies you believe would be interested in you and by whom you can imagine being employed. Now what? How do you actually reach out and connect with these companies so they can learn how great you really are?

how to market yourself

Chapter 10

The next step in landing a job
is figuring out how to introduce
you, the MPC, to the people
who can hire you. You'll need to
figure out who the person is within
the company who is most likely to
hire someone like you - the person
who will ultimately sit across
from you and decide,
"I want you to work for me."

10

Developing A Plan To Contact Companies

In the recruiting field, we call this person the hiring authority. It could be the president, a vice president, a manager, a director, or people who hold an array of other titles. Believe it or not, seldom is this person the HR Coordinator, Representative, Administrator or Assistant. At the risk of sounding harsh (and remember, my degree is in HR), it's doubtful anyone in HR is going to make the final hiring decision (unless, of course, you are interviewing for a position within the HR department).

> So why does almost everyone think the best way to get a job at a company is to send a resume to someone in HR?

It's a pattern of behavior. That's all.

We've been conditioned to put together a resume, then send it off to HR. The reality, though, is that this is probably the least likely way to get you an audience with your potential next employer.

Let's look at HR's function. Historically speaking, HR (or Personnel as it was called when I got my degree) was the keeper of records. They were administrators. They maintained the employee records for management. Then as the world of business evolved, and employees' needs became more complex and became more of a conscious consideration for top management, HR expanded its power beyond simple record keeping. Benefits needed to be administered, employee relations issues needed tending, terminations, layoffs, retirements and many other employee "transactions" needed to be processed. Among these employee transactions fell hiring. <u>HR became the coordinator of the hiring process</u>. Placing advertisements or postings and contacting recruiters were among some of the strategies HR would use to fulfill the recruitment requirements. They would gather resumes and begin the arduous process of selection.

The selection process also drew the attention of these new HR practitioners. Line managers turned to HR to assist them in determining what the necessary requirements were of a particular job, and the more progressive HR practitioners would even counsel company managers on matters such as effective interviewing. HR became the facilitators of the hiring process - gathering information about candidates through reference checks, testing skills, and helping the ultimate decision-maker bring the best candidate forward.

But the common thread since the beginning of time is that HR practitioners (like external recruiters) are facilitators of the process. They are NOT the final decision makers 99% of the time. And I say 99% of the time because people do need to be hired into HR departments, so every now and then HR gets to be the final hiring authority. So what does this mean to you the job seeker? Recognize the importance of HR, but recognize it for what it is. Do you have to please HR and work with and through them in a cooperative vein? Yes. <u>But do you necessarily want them to be your point of entry when it comes to determining if you want to pursue a career with a particular company?</u> I think not.

So who do you contact? How do you get your foot in the proverbial door? I am going to ask you again to think outside of what you know to be the usual.

Think.

Think as if _you_ were going to hire you. What position would you hold? You already know the positions you are qualified for and the positions you are interested in, right? Now think about who the person is who is most likely to hire you. It is probably the person who is most likely to sign your performance appraisal and do your review.

Let's look at some examples:

Your Position's Title	Your Boss' Title
Sales Rep	Sales Manager
Sales Manager	Director of Sales or VP of Sales
Staff Accountant	CFO or VP of Finance
Secretary	Director of Administration
Executive Secretary	CEO, President or VP
Project Coordinator	Program Manager
Receptionist	Office Manager or Executive Assistant

Are you getting the drift? Look at your history. Who are the people you have reported to? These are probably the people who will make the ultimate decision as to whether or not you get hired. So why not talk to them?

But you may say, "But what if I talk to the sales manager, and he says there are no openings?" I say, "What is the purpose of your call?" (Remember our earlier discussion about the purpose of your call?) You may not stumble across an opening at this company with this manager at this time, but by having an intelligent conversation with someone in the position to hire you at one company, you are much more likely to be referred to someone of equal stature and level of hiring authority at, say, another organization.

Remember. . . People Talk!

Business professionals talk about what's going on in their companies with other people. Ask the manager who he knows who he can connect you with. What's the worst thing that can happen? He says he doesn't know anyone. Then what can you do? How about asking him for his advice? Everyone loves to help someone and *everyone* loves to give advice. (You've heard the saying about opinions, right?

The same goes for advice.) Let him know what you've done so far to source new companies. Ask him if he has any ideas on emerging companies, suppliers, vendors, customers, competitors who might be interested in talking with someone with your experience. You will be *amazed* at the response you get, when you move beyond the level of asking if there are any openings. Now, worst case, this person knows nothing - no one, no companies. Then what do you do? I would recommend closing by thanking him for his time, and asking him if you may call him in the future. Try to leave the door open for future networking.

Consider **who** you will ask for and **what** you may likely hear from him or her.

Title	How can they possibly help you?
Line Manager	
An Assistant	
Human Resources	
Other Departments	

So by now you know who you are, what you want, what companies you are going to contact, and who within those companies you are going to ask for.

But what do you say?

Developing A Pitch Or Presentation

One of the first tasks I was given on my first day as a recruiter was to develop a feature/benefit presentation for my MPC. I sat in the company's conference room with another trainee who wrote feverishly on a piece of legal paper as my mind drew a complete blank. When my new boss walked in, I asked for her assistance. You see, I wasn't a sales person. I was an HR professional. I had not the first clue about selling anything, and now my livelihood depended on it. So I made the decision to get a clue. And here's what I learned.

Determining The Goal Of Your Call

Because I'm a person who needs a framework within which to work, I needed to <u>know what the goal of my phone call would be</u>. You too need to have an end in mind before you start out. Let's look at your goal. Oh that's right! It's to get a job! And the fastest way to get a job is to be interviewed by a company that is hiring someone just like you. So your primary goal of making a presentation call is to land your candidate an interview. (In the recruiting world, we call this getting a Send Out.)

But what if you don't land an interview? Is your call for naught? Are you a failure? Should you give up? The answer to all three questions is an unequivocal **"no."**

If your call doesn't result in you becoming a "Send out," then set your sites on achieving another goal. One of the best pieces of advice I received from a recruiting manager was to get something out of each call. I was instructed to make sure that by the time I hung up the phone (or in some cases, the phone was hung up on me!) I had received something of value. You too can receive something of value for each call if you choose to look for the good. Finding the positive outcome for each call will also provide you with motivation to make the next call, and the next call and the next call.

What are some other goals you can achieve during your call?

Other Goals Of The Call

When you hang up the phone and still haven't secured an interview, what else can you learn or obtain that will let you know your call was a success?

Other Opportunities *(the alternative job order or job opening)*

Is the company hiring someone in a different area?

How would you find out this information?

Fact Finding *(learning more about the industry/company/position/etc.)*

You can find information about the company or learn about the people within the company who hold your position. This information will make you more knowledgeable overall and will give you things to talk about with other employers. It will broaden your frame of reference. It will also let the employer know you are not operating in a vacuum or being tunnel-visioned. You will also demonstrate your ability to see outside the box and explore other possibilities. The information you gather will help you get to the next step. Maybe a question you ask sparks an interest in the person on the other end of the phone.

Here's an example: When I marketed a particular candidate and seemed to get little or no positive response, I would step outside of the sales role and engage the hiring manager in a conversation that meant something to them. For instance, I might say something like this after finding out they had no opening: "Can I please ask your opinion on something?" Almost every time, the answer is yes. We all love to be asked for our opinion and love even more to share it! I would go on to say, "I have not found the right opportunity for the person I just described, and I'm wondering if you could help me understand why." The person will usually tell me what's going on in their company that is preventing them from hiring. Whatever the answer is, I now have something else to talk about. So if it's "We just aren't hiring," I might ask, "Is that because of the market, or is it because you don't have turnover?" Again, no matter what the answer is, you have something to talk about. Perhaps they say, "We just haven't had turnover." You can respond with, "That must mean you are a great company to work for - the type of company I would be looking for. What would be the best way for me to stay connected with you should an opening arise for someone with my skills and experience?" **I'm telling you, no other applicant is doing this!!** No other applicant is looking ahead to the long term. No other applicant is considering the likelihood that they could work for this company even though there is no opening at the moment. No other applicant is speaking **the language of possibilities.**

Most applicants are speaking the language of grim reality. They don't have an opening. I'll never find a job. They don't need anyone like me. If these are your thoughts, this will be your reality. "Your thoughts become things." I've seen it time and again. You can choose to focus on the temporary grimness of your current reality and keep it happening, or you can shift your focus and conversations to the possibilities of getting what you want.

Following Up

Another goal of your call may be to follow up - either on a resume you have sent or to follow up after you have had an interview. I get asked by many people what the "rule" is for following up. How soon after you send a resume should you follow up to make sure your resume was received? How soon after you interview should you follow up to find out if you are still in the running?

While there is no hard and fast rule that dictates the appropriate amount of time a job applicant should wait before making a follow up call, I would consider a few things before picking up the phone. First, how did you come to hear about the opening? If you sent your resume in response to a posting you saw online, or if you answered an advertisement, or if your resume is one of thousands an employer received from some outbound mass communication, don't waste your time making a follow up call. Remember: As I mentioned before, it's a numbers game. You are but one of many resumes being considered and the chance of your resume being selected is not great. And the chance of your receiving a positive response from the overwhelmed Human Resources representative charged with the daunting task of sifting through several hundred resumes is less than zero.

But what if you have sent your resume based upon a personal or professional referral? How long should you then wait for a response? I would let common sense rule. If you send your resume on a Monday and do not receive a response by Friday, make the call. If you connect with the hiring manager or the Human Resources representative, simply let them know you are following up to ensure your resume has been received. If you find that the resume has been received, it is acceptable to ask about next steps if the person you are calling doesn't offer that information. How do you ask about next steps? Simply ask, "When would it be appropriate for me to follow up with you?" They will appreciate not being forced to give you a specific deadline. (Remember, they are BUSY!)

Following up after an interview really depends upon how things were left at the close of an interview. At the end of your interview, what was said about next steps? If nothing was said, did you ask? If you did not ask about next steps, then unfortunately, you have created a situation where you will have to live with the employer's timing – not yours. And calling an employer to ask if you are still in the running could be interpreted as annoying at worst and desperate at best. Better to send a thank you letter after the interview than to make a follow up phone call that will potentially irritate the person who can hire you.

Obtaining Referrals

When you talk to someone who doesn't have an opening suited to you, perhaps he or she knows someone who you might like to meet with. That referral may be someone else within the company or it might be someone within his or her network or sphere of influence. Let's break this down.

Let's say you are talking to an HR manager who says, "We don't have any openings." You might ask, "Do you know of anyone within the company I might connect with who would have an interest in my skills and experience?" She might say no to this question as well. She is thinking in her box called "my company" or her box called "the situation I find myself in at the moment I received your call." But what about the people she knows *outside* her company? What about the ideas she has that are *outside* of her current situation? How do you get this person to help you get to the next place?

Consider asking some of these questions:

> Are you a part of any professional organizations?

Human Resources professionals oftentimes belong to a local chapter of the Society of Human Resource Management (SHRM).

> Can you recommend a community group?

People in leadership positions often belong to community based organizations like Rotary, Optimists, Chambers of Commerce, etc. These groups host events that are open to guests and are tremendous sources for networking.

"Do you participate in any formal networking groups?"

Sales professionals typically promote their businesses through formal networking groups. You have heard of BNI (Business Networking International). I belong to a Michigan-based networking group called LBN (Local Business Network). While it may not make sense to attend one of these meetings yourself, ask the referral source to connect you with people in their networking group who can talk to about your next position. Remember, you're not asking this person to place you in a job... you're simply asking them to introduce you to someone you can network with.

Next, how can you connect with the people who can hire you other than by making calls?

Networking 101:

Making warm or cold calls directly to companies is a great way to connect with potential jobs and the people who can get you hired. But there are other methods to connect with people who can help you in your search. How can you do this? Networking. But what is networking? How do you do it? And who do you do it with?

Networking Defined

According to Merriam Webster, networking is defined as follows:

"the exchange of information or services among individuals, groups, or institutions; specifically: the cultivation of productive relationships for employment or business."

Most people are very uncomfortable with the idea of networking. They think networking will require them to be someone other than who they really are (i.e. a salesperson) and to do something they don't feel qualified to do (i.e. sell). I understand their hesitation. When I was just beginning my career, my colleagues talked about networking, and my first thought was "how contrived is that?' and my second thought was, "why should I have to spend time with a bunch of people I may not want to be with?" It was several years into my career before I truly understood the power (and pleasure!) of networking.

When I advise job seekers to tap into their network to land a job, I am often met with either a glazed look or a full blown objection. They say things like:

> **My network doesn't know anyone hiring.**

This is a pretty big assumption. As a coach, one of my jobs is to help my clients test assumptions. Because when you make an assumption, you have a 50% chance of being wrong. So how can you test your assumption that no one within your sphere of influence knows anyone who is hiring? You can ask them. You can actually reach out and ask who they know who might be in a position to help you in your career search.

> **The people in my network aren't in the same line of work as me.**

This is another objection job seekers often voice. This objection is based upon the assumption that only people who are involved in your line of work can help you connect with a new job. The truth is that normally the person who will help you get to your next job is not the person you are directly associated with, but one of the people they know. Your friend will most likely not find you a job, but someone in your friend's network could very well connect you with an opportunity. It's not always your network that will get the result you want; more often it's your friend's network that holds the greater possibilities for success.

"I would feel really awkward asking people in my network to find me a job." Many people feel they are imposing upon their friends, family, colleagues, etc. by asking for help in their job search. But begging people you know to help you get back to work is not networking. Let's return to Webster's definition.

Networking involves the "exchange of information or services." Tapping into your network to obtain information that will help you move forward in your search is different from begging for a job. There is a distinct difference in the following requests:

> "I just got laid off. Can you help me find a job?"

This question, as I mentioned before, sounds like begging. It puts the person you are networking with on the spot – especially if they CANNOT help you find a job. By asking this question, you are also expecting your friend or colleague to figure out how they can help you, and in my experience, this places an unreasonable amount of responsibility on the person to determine exactly how they can help you. What if that person doesn't know how to help you find a job? What if that person has never had to look for a job? What if that person doesn't know what you do? You'll likely get a response that, although empathetic, offers you no next step.

> "I'm involved in a career search. Can you help me connect with people who I can talk with about who I am and what I do?"

This question starts out with a more positive tone. You aren't 'looking for a job,' but are involved in a career search. It sounds more proactive from the start. It also sets the stage for an exchange of information vs. a cry for help. Next, by asking your friend to help you connect with someone, you are letting them off the hook by not expecting them to find you a job. You are also not assuming they know what you do for a living. You are specifically asking them for a connection to someone who might be open to talking with you about who you are and what you do. You are also giving your friend or colleague a concrete way they can help you.

Cultivating Productive Relationships

The greatest by-product of networking is the cultivation of productive relationships. It is a known fact that people do business with people they know, like and trust. Networking allows you, the job seeker, to get to know people. And as you build these relationships, as people get the opportunity to learn more about you, they will naturally want to help you in your search.

Who Do I Network With And Where Do I do It?

You'll want to build relationships with people who are somehow connected to the profession or job you are after. For instance, if you are an engineer, you'll want to network among other engineers. Why? Other engineers may know of companies that have a need for your services or may know of trends within companies that employ people like you. Other engineers who have been involved in job searches may be able to share best practices with you that might make your search more efficient. Where do you find people who are connected to your profession? Professional associations are a great place to start. And what are the goals of these organizations? Typically, to provide their members with opportunities to cultivate productive relationships with one another.

But what if you are not among the "professional" ranks? What if there aren't associations (or you are not aware of associations) designed for people in your line of work? Where can you go to network? I would recommend taking a look at the industries within which you have worked or the industries within which you would like to work. What types of groups have been formed by people in these industries? There are groups formed by people in advertising, automotive, accounting, construction... the list goes on. Find out where these groups meet, visit their websites, see what they're up to, and get involved. You'll be amazed at the relationships you will forge.

Networking is also something that can be done outside a formal networking setting. Talk with your former employers and coworkers. Where are they? What are they up to? Who do they know? Talk with people in your family and neighborhood, and check in frequently with your friends. You may be surprised how many resources you may have overlooked that are very close to you. *(I am stunned by how few calls I get from friends and close colleagues who are involved in a job search. And I'm a career coach!)* So don't forget to consider your network that is closest to you.

Online Social Networking

Online social networking is a fairly new phenomenon, but baby boomers (like me) are slowly adapting to this new way of connecting. If you are looking for a job and have not tapped into the available online networking sites, it's time to get started. If you don't know what it's about, go on line and check out the hundreds of free seminars available on how to get the most out of these online networking tools. When you are looking for a job, especially in a crummy economy, you need to employ every tool possible. And that means enduring the discomfort of learning how to do things you've never done before.

What To Do When Your Networking Results In A Referral

Let's say the manager with whom you connected gives you the name of someone they think you should talk to. Then what do you do? How do you approach this person? What is your goal?

> The **greatest** by-product of networking is the cultivation of *productive relationships*

Lead in with the referral source. "Hi, Jim. Jane Doe at ABC suggested I contact you. Is this a good time to talk?" (It's always a nice gesture to ask a busy executive whether they are available to speak. If they aren't, respect that, and close by asking for a time to follow up.)

Now let's say Jim says it's an OK time to talk. Then what? You're going to go in with your pitch. For instance: "My name is Therese. I am currently in the process of a career search, and I need your help. I am a _____who does_____ and is looking for _____. How do you feel someone with this type of experience and talent might fit within your organization?" (Notice I'm NOT asking if he has an opening! I'm asking him to imagine how I might fit within his company. If he can imagine this he will more likely be able to refer me to someone who will also be likely to see me fitting into his company.)

Remember, you have been referred to Jim by someone, so it is pretty likely that there is some level of fit. Jim is probably going to say, "You know, your experience does sound good, and you might be a fit for our organization, but we just don't have any openings at this time." Then what do you do?

Well if you're like 99% of the job seeking population, your shoulders drop, your smile quickly fades, and your mind says, "I knew it. I'll never find a job." You probably then thank Jim for his time, and hang up the phone and let this feeling of rejection settle into your bones. You don't pick up the phone again until the feeling fades… maybe in a couple days or a couple hours. And then when you do pick up the phone, you prepare yourself for the next proverbial kick in the teeth.

<u>OK, is it possible to present another more positive and productive strategy?</u> Let's go back. Let's say Jim says, "You know, your experience does sound good, and you might be a fit for our organization, but we just don't have any openings at this time." You might say, "Really! What is it about my experience that seems like a fit?" or "I'm glad to know you feel my skills and experience are a fit for an organization like ABC. When your company is hiring (and you know one day they will!) what types of people do you envision them looking for?" or, "When you find yourself ready to hire someone, what are some of the

things your company looks for?" There are plenty of positive, forward-moving questions you can ask in response to an employer's statement.

Exercise:

What are some possible responses or questions you may have to these?

Your experience sounds good, but we don't have a need for someone like you at this time:

_____

_____

_____

We only look for people with _____ experience (which you don't have):

_____

_____

I heard that ABC was looking for someone like you:

_____

_____

Putting Together Your Pitch

Now that you know the possible goals of your call, we can take a look at how to craft a pitch or a feature/benefit presentation that will accurately convey what's important about you and hopefully capture the interest of your prospective employer.

First, get out a piece of paper.
Now, on that piece of paper, make a large "T".

Now label the T-Chart as follows

Features	Benefits

Now comes the fun part. You get to fill in the blanks. This brainstorming exercise is the first step in developing a great pitch.

Let's start with your features... what makes you a great candidate?

What will an employer learn about you either from looking at your resume or from meeting you that will make them want to hire you?

Is it;   your experience?

your skills?

your education?

your interpersonal skills?

your character strengths?

Go ahead and list them all. If you have trouble thinking of what your great features are, ask someone! Call up one of the people who knows you - or better, ask someone who's worked with you.

Next comes a trickier part. You've got to *look carefully at each feature that makes you great,* and you have to *determine how that feature is a benefit to your prospective employer.* How does that strength translate into a benefit the employer will receive?

Let's look at an easy example:

Feature: 12 years' experience working for a manufacturing company
Benefit: Able to assimilate quickly and apply this knowledge for a new manufacturing company

Feature: Extremely reliable, good attendance
Benefit: Company can rest assured their attendance rate will be positively impacted by hiring you

Feature: I type 100 words per minute
Benefit: I can produce a very high volume of work in a short period of time

Why is it important to state the obvious?

When I was a recruiter trainee (or a "rookie" as we were so lovingly called), I found it hard to believe that I had to state the obvious. Come on...! If I type 100 words per minute, *obviously* I can do twice as much work as someone who types 50 words per minute. Can't the potential employer make this mental leap just as easily as I can? Probably. But will he? Your job (as was mine) is to demonstrate quickly and clearly what's in it for him - why he should talk to you or hire you.

You have to paint a clear picture.

Focusing on What's Important

One of the things that made me super successful in my recruiting practice was my ability to properly present my candidate's strengths. And I focused on making my presentation meaningful by learning what was important to my client (the hiring company) and to my candidate (the applicant).

30-Second Commercial

You've heard it called the elevator speech or the 60 second commercial right? All the experts say you need to get your speech down. You've got to commit to memory what you want people to know about you so you make the best possible first impression.

I agree that the pitch is powerful. It's your lead in. It's just like your handshake. It can pave the way for a meaningful conversation or it can shut the door on a great opportunity. But how do you create a good pitch? Especially if you aren't a "salesperson," how do you craft the ideal presentation?

First, cut it in half. Make it 30 seconds and not the 60 seconds most of the books recommend. Why? 60 seconds is a LONG time. Get out a watch with a second hand and see for yourself.

When the second hand hits the 12, say, "Hello, my name is_____, and I am a
_____." Now wait until the second hand hits the 12 again. Do you think you
can fill up all that time with features and benefits about you? Do you think you will
hold the attention of your listener? In today's world of information overload, less is
more and your audience will more likely process and retain a quick message than a
lengthy infomercial.

Your 30-second commercial needs to convey 4 things:

1 Who you are and what you do (your background)

2 What you are good at (your features)

3 What that means to a potential employer (the benefits)

4 What you are looking for (your objective)

Who you are and what you do (background)...

Start by briefly describing your recent employment background and tenure. If you
feel your schooling is important, then mention your degree. If you're not sure where
to start, take a look at your resume. All this information is there, so get to know that
document intimately.

Who I am and what I do:

_____

_____

_____

What you are good at (features)...

Next, state any of the accomplishments you've achieved during your career or highlight any personal features you feel an employer may be attracted to. To find this information, revisit your SWOT analysis.

What I am good at is:

_____

_____

_____

What it means to an employer (benefits)...

Now, imagine how a prospective employer could benefit by having you on their team. What benefits will they potentially experience as a result of your features? Take a look at the "opportunities" section of your SWOT analysis and you will likely find this information.

What this means to an employer is:

_____

_____

_____

What you're looking for (objective)...

And last, close with where you see yourself fitting in – what position, department, industry or specific companies. Let your audience know what your goal is...and how they can help you reach your goal. If you're not clear on your goal, revisit the exercise where you designed the "Ideal Position."

I'm looking for:

_____

_____

_____

Putting It All Together

Now, put these four statements together, and say it all out loud. I would recommend saying it out loud alone first. Then, say it out loud, alone, and in front of a mirror. And then say it out loud and in the presence of a trusted friend or colleague - someone who will offer you honest and constructive feedback. In any event – PRACTICE! It may sound elementary, but the only way to make an effective presentation of ANY kind is to practice. And when you're looking for a job it's imperative. Your livelihood depends on it.

Who I am and what I do:

What I am good at:

What this means to an employer is:

I'm looking for:

giving good **phone**

Chapter 11

When I began my solo recruiting
practice, I had to invest in a lot of
tools that would allow me to run a
successful business. The tool that
I spent the most money on was the
tool that would allow me to connect
with as many potential hiring
managers as possible -
my telephone.

11

Anatomy Of The Call

Should you choose to use the telephone as your means of communication - and I hope you will consider it - there is a fundamental formula I used for 20-some years that reaped some great benefits. In the following paragraphs I will explore the anatomy of a successful marketing call. But first, here are the components:

> Introducing yourself
>
> Confirming you are talking with the right person
>
> Making a request for assistance
>
> Giving the presentation of your features and benefits
>
> Closing for the next step

Introduction: Making The Right Impression

When you make phone calls, you'll need to introduce yourself to the person on the other end of the line, and you'll want to introduce yourself with confidence, clarity and a positive tone. If you have prepared for the call - that is, you know who you are calling, are clear on your objective, and have done the work to design a successful pitch or presentation - then you are ready to introduce yourself with confidence and deliver a clear message.

But What's So Important About A Positive Tone?

When you speak on the phone, the most striking feature of your call is not so much the content of your pitch, but the method of delivery. Employers will pick up on whatever tone you are using - *positive or negative*. It's important to be in a positive mindset prior to picking up the phone. Make sure your voice projects positive energy. If you aren't sure if you're emitting the right tone, call your own voicemail, and leave your pitch. How do you sound? Do you sound engaged? Engaging? Interested? Interesting? Would you want to talk further to you? Would you be energized by talking with you? Or de-energized? Be honest with yourself. And make adjustments in your attitude if you need to before you go on to the next call. Back in my recruiting days, I would keep a mirror on my desk. Before I made a call, I would look at myself (and normally crack up, or at least crack a smile) and then make sure the look on my face was positive. If my face looked positive, I could be more certain my tone would follow suit.

Exercise:

Take a look at yourself in the mirror as you talk on the phone, and what do you notice:

> When you are talking with a friend making social plans?
>
> When you are on hold for a very long time?
>
> When you are talking to a telemarketer?
>
> When you are tracking down your kids?
>
> When you are talking with your credit card company?
>
> When you are talking with a coworker?
>
> When you are talking to a potential employer?

Confirming You've Reached The Right Person

How do you know if you're talking with the right person? The one who can help you connect with a potential job opportunity? How about asking? Remember, you have already done some research, right? You know the title of the individual you need to talk with:

It sounds like this:

Phone gets answered:	"Hello, this is Jim Smith."
You say:	"Hello, Jim, are you the VP of Marketing?"

Not so hard, is it? If he says, **"Yes,"** continue with your call. If he says, **"No,"** ask him, **"Who is?"**

People make this step much harder than it really is. They feel they have to go into lots of information with the person who picks up the phone. I say, less is more. Your goal is to connect with the right person, so don't spend too much time talking with people who cannot further your progress in the search for a new position.

Request For Assistance

As a recruiter for executive assistants to CEOs, I found that asking for assistance got me great results. And I learned with time, that just about everyone I connected with was interested in helping me if I would ask for that help. Picking up the conversation where we just left off (I have confirmed that I have the right person on the line), here's how I would ask for help:

Jim says:	"Yes, I'm the VP of Marketing."
You say:	"Great, I need your help. Do you have a moment?"

Like I said, most people will stop when they hear a request for help. I also followed up with a quick acknowledgment that Jim could be busy, and asked if he had a moment to talk. I used "moment" because I want Jim to know that I respect his time and don't plan on keeping him on the phone too long.

Presentation Of Features/Benefits

Once I have Jim's attention, I give the pitch I have developed that I feel will be most attractive to someone in Jim's position.

Closing For The Next Step:

Once I complete my presentation, I end with a close. I end with a question that will potentially move this call forward. What are some possible closes?

To Get An Interview:

"Would you be open to meeting with me to discuss career opportunities within your organization?"

To Get An Internal Referral:

"Whom do you know within your organization who might be interested in meeting with me to discuss career opportunities?"

To Get An External Referral:

"Whom do you know within another organization like yours who might be interested in meeting with me to discuss career opportunities?"

What are some other closes that would move you forward? Is it possible that Jim is part of some associations you might want to become a part of? Is it possible for you to ask Jim his opinion on what's going on in your field? Could you potentially begin to develop a relationship with Jim? Closing doesn't have to be an offer or an interview. Closing is asking a question that engages the person and moves you forward in your search.

working **YOUR** plan

Chapter 12

You're probably figuring out by now that finding a job *is* a job. And it's a sales job that requires daily activity. Successful salespeople – or successful recruiters – become successful because they know how to create a plan, execute their plan, and measure their results.

12

You will land a job if you set specific goals for job search activity. You cannot control what your results are, but you can certainly control what your level of activity is. You can also learn from the activity if you take the time to review what you have done, what has worked, what has not worked.

When I was at the peak of my recruiting success, I found that my planning and goal-setting time was the most valuable time of my day, week and month. But what sorts of activity should you be tracking, measuring and analyzing?

The number of:

calls you are making

people you are connecting with

voicemail messages you are leaving

emails you are sending

resumes you are sending

posting sites you are reviewing

conversations you are having with hiring managers

networking sites you are updating

meetings/networking functions you are attending

people you are talking with about your job search

Notice that all of these are activities you have control over.

When you sit down to make phone calls, **don't set this goal**: "Today, I am going to find a job." You may find one, or you may not.

Rather, **set this goal:** "I am going to make 10 calls to hiring managers." When you complete these 10 calls, you will feel a sense of accomplishment and will maintain a positive level of motivation regardless of whether you identify an opening. Activity naturally brings results. So stay active by working your plan.

Set Daily, Weekly, And Monthly Goals

Each day you are looking for a job, you will have recurring activities that you'll need to complete. Checking posting sites, updating your online profiles on the social networking sites, researching, etc. These passive activities, while they may not bring immediate (or predictable) results, need to be carried out on a daily basis.

Develop a list of daily activities you plan to complete:

Daily Activity   **Amount of Time**

_____   _____

_____   _____

_____   _____

_____   _____

_____   _____

_____   _____

Take a look at the activities. What percentage of your time are you spending on passive strategies and what percentage are you spending on active strategies? Remember, more than 70% of all jobs are found via active strategies (networking, etc.). Are you spending your search time wisely? How much time are you spending each day looking for a job? Be honest. Looking for a job is a full time job! If you are spending a couple hours a day scouring the classifieds and scanning the Internet, what are you doing the rest of the day?

Start to track your activities. Every successful recruiter keeps a record of what they have done so they know what results they can expect. In the years that I was recruiting, I tracked every phone call I made, every person I sent out on an interview, every job opening I worked on and every placement I made.

Looking for a job is a numbers game. The higher the numbers, the greater the likelihood of getting hired. The more people you talk with, the more likely that you will connect with the person who can hire you. Work the numbers. Make the calls. And watch the results.

On the next page is a sample Job Search Planner. Use it as a guide to develop a written planner that works for you that you can use each day.

Sample Job Search Planner

Date	Company	Person Contacted Title	Phone Number / Email	Result / Comments

Just Make The First Call

In the life of a successful recruiter, the most difficult task is making the first call.

Think about it: You've done your planning. You know your product "You", you know your market, and you know who to ask for. You know what you want. But you don't know what is going to happen when you make that first connection. Will the person be helpful? Will they be irritated? Will they be discouraging? The 'will they' questions will spin so fast through your mind, you will be compelled to do nothing until you have imagined every possible scenario and how you might want to react to it. This state is commonly called "paralysis through analysis." It happens when you are so focused on what could happen, that you forget to make anything happen. But this is your career. This is your livelihood. You'll need to force yourself to make that first call. You may even need to trick yourself into making the second call. But I guarantee that by the time you have made the 10th consecutive call, you will forget how anxious you had been before you got started.

And yes, I said 10 consecutive calls. There is a certain momentum or rhythm that comes through repetition. Many job seekers are inclined to hear one, two or three objections or "no's" and hang up the phone, bemoan their situation, and conclude there are no jobs to be had. They make general statements like, "I made some calls and didn't find a position." Or "There's just nothing happening out there." Three calls - or even ten calls is not enough data for you to draw any conclusions other than that you need to make more calls.

So how many calls is enough?

As many as it takes for you to move to the next step. As many as it takes for you to get an interview. To get a meeting with someone who can help get you to the next place. To get information that will help you get to the next place.

When I was beginning my recruiting career - as you are right now - it was a tough time. The unemployment rate in Michigan was nearly as high as it is today. I'm telling you, I had plenty of reason to complain that there were no jobs out there! Funny, though, that during the early 1990's when Michigan's unemployment rate was the worst in the country, I was consistently in the top 10 account executives within my recruiting company. Nationally! I beat out individuals who were in markets much richer than Southeastern Michigan's. Why? Because I didn't buy into the fact that there were no jobs out there. I kept making calls until I found an opportunity to get my MPC an interview.

But how do you keep yourself motivated in the face of discouragement?

I found (and still find!) many ways to stay motivated during challenging times. What will work for you depends on you. And how well you know you.

It's very likely that **you** are getting in the way of landing the job of your dreams.

This may be tough to swallow, but it is very possible you are sabotaging your success without even realizing it. Now I'm not saying you are doing this on purpose. What I'm saying is that each of us runs programs in our mind that run our lives unless we become conscious of the programs and purposefully set out to reverse the negative patterns.

So how do you know if there is a negative pattern preventing you from getting to your next job? Start listening to your responses to the questions people ask you about your search. When people ask you how your job search is going, do you hear yourself saying things like:

"I can't find anything in my field."

"There's nothing out there."

"No one is hiring people like me."

"I can't get the salary I need."

"I'm overqualified for everything I apply for."

"I'm going to have to take a pay cut to land a job."

There is a Universal Law called the "Law of Attraction." That phrase, although used widely by esoteric writers, does not have an agreed-upon definition. However, the general consensus among New Thought thinkers is that the Law of Attraction takes the principal "Like Attracts Like" and applies it to conscious desire. That is,

A person's thoughts (conscious and unconscious), emotions, and beliefs cause a change in the physical world that attracts positive or negative experiences that correspond to the aforementioned thoughts, with or without the person taking action to attain such experiences.

This process has been described as "harmonious vibrations of the law of attraction," or "you get what you think about; your thoughts determine your experience."

So if your mantra is "I can't find anything in my field," guess what? You aren't going to find anything in your field. If your thought and belief is "No one is hiring someone like me," then you will remain unemployed. I remember very well a time when "no one" was using a recruiter for hiring clerical employees - especially here in Michigan where we were experiencing close to 10% unemployment. The common thought was

"Why should I pay a recruiter to find me applicants? There are tons of people who would be happy to take the job I am advertising." During this time, I attended a regional conference held in Columbus, Ohio, where the CEO of the recruiting firm I worked for made a statement that turned my thoughts from gloom to boom. He said that if you want to achieve the same results you achieved during the good years, you'll have to exert about 25% more effort during this challenging year. Doing things the same way you've done them before will result in backsliding. In order to put forth 25% more effort though, I would have to look for hiring opportunities with more earnest and with greater momentum. I set my intention to make at least 25% more calls.

As I made these calls I would hear things like this from the person on the other end of the phone: "No one's hiring," "If we were to hire, we wouldn't use a recruiter," "Times are tough," "We're in a recession." It may sound simple, but I assumed the attitude one of my teammates would so eloquently say in response to these naysayers. "We have chosen not to acknowledge the recession that our competitors are talking about. We are very busy in our office filling positions with lots of successful companies." Now was this true at that moment? It was probably a bit of a stretch. We *were* busy in our office - busy finding opportunities we could work on. But you know what happened? By consciously not buying in to the attitude of defeat and by focusing on the possibility that we could rise above the current economic situation, we did move forward. And in 1991, my positive-minded colleague was named National Rookie of the Year, and I found myself in the nation's Top Ten Account Executives - both awards granted to people working in a region where there were *no jobs*! How did that happen? By focusing on the possibility of success despite economic indicators.

So what are some practical things you can do to keep your focus on the positive? To set your intention on the good things that are happening? My recommendation is to have a plan you can work automatically. Build a plan you don't need to think about to execute it successfully. Work this plan blindly each day. Make your completion of the calls your measure of success.

Going back again to my time as a rookie account executive, I would often start my day with the goal of finding a job opening (or in recruiter lingo… getting a job order).

If at the end of the day, I had not written a new job order, I felt like a failure. I'd build another plan for the next day, make the calls, and would quite possibly have the same result: No job order. I was making 20, 40, 50, sometimes 60 calls per day, and I wasn't writing a job order! How hopeless was that?

Then one day during a team meeting we talked about our goals. I proudly stated, "My goal is to get a job order today." And my manager, in her wisdom asked, "Do you have any control over whether or not you happen to call a company that happens to have a job opening and then happens to want to work with a recruiter?" I thought for a moment, and then realized I was setting myself up for failure. I was setting my goal based upon something I couldn't possibly control. At that moment, I shifted my way of thinking. My new goal became more realistic. I said, "My goal is to call forty companies on behalf of my MPC." You see, recruiting (like job hunting) is a numbers game. If you make the calls, you will find the opportunity. It's a given. So I began to focus on the calls. At the end of the day, I could feel a sense of accomplishment. I had achieved the goal I had set out to accomplish. I had made 40 calls. I knew that if I kept making this volume of calls, it was just a matter of time before I would land my MPC in a position.

But there's another pitfall you'll need to be aware of if you determine to subscribe to this line of thought and action. Let's say you land an opportunity – someone has an opening and they want to meet with you. Don't STOP!!! It is human nature to stop and put all our eggs into that one basket. Remember: It's a numbers game. **Keep making calls. Keep looking for opportunity**. Give yourself the luxury of choosing between a couple of job options, rather than jumping right into the first opportunity that comes your way.

So now you've taken you, the MPC, to market. And if you have done it right, you've gotten yourself an appointment. You've become a "Send Out." (This is the recruiter term for a person going out on an interview.) What do you need to have in place before you arrive at the meeting?

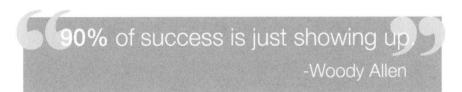

90% of success is just showing up.

-Woody Allen

before you INTERVIEW

Chapter 13

While I don't want to minimize the importance of having a well crafted resume, in my opinion, this strategy is about as effective as standing on your front porch and hollering "I need a job" at the top of your lungs and expecting a passing car to stop and offer you a position at the driver's company.

13

Presenting Yourself Well On Paper
Resume Preparation

Notice that my comments on resumes do NOT appear at the beginning of this book. Most people involved in a job search think that creating the perfect resume will land them the perfect job. They believe the first step in a job search is to put together a nice looking, politically and corporately correct piece of paper and then start sending it out to employers to see what comes in.

I'm not saying resumes are unimportant, but I think the goal of a resume should NOT be to land you a job. Rather a <u>resume's goal is to accurately convey to an employer what you have done that might mean something to them</u>. The importance of your resume during the job search is just to show a potential employer <u>what you have done in the past</u>. That's IT! It isn't designed to *get* you in the door; it's there to help you remember everything you've done during your career, so you can explain it to the hiring manager once you are already in the door.

Resumes, in all honesty, are used by employers to weed you out, not to weed you *in*. HR people do not sift through the hundreds of resumes that flood their email accounts and mailboxes saying, "Now how can I make this person fit into our organization?" No, their thought processes more accurately go something like this: "How do I reduce this very large stack of resumes to a group of 10-15 pieces of paper I will read more carefully?" I'm telling you, your resume is probably the worst way to land an interview. But if you are one of the lucky ones who is selected - if you win the resume lottery - there are probably some things you did right to avoid being eliminated from the running.

There are some resume realities that I've come to know in the last 20+ years. Here are my guidelines on resumes, Spartan as they may seem;

Keep It Simple And Accurate

There are many opinions on what makes a great resume. I am asked over and over again, "Does the format of a resume matter?" or "Can you look at my resume and give me your opinion?" Honestly, I think a resume is just about the worst way to market a person. Because resumes are used as tools to weed you *out*, no matter how beautiful your resume, there is still a very strong likelihood something on it will trigger the employer to eliminate you from the running. My opinion of resumes?

I believe the very best resume is NOT the one that impresses the most; rather, it is the one that <u>offends the least</u>.

Cover Letters

As with resumes, there have been volumes of materials written about cover letters. What kind of paper should they be written on? How long or how short should they be? Should they be formal or informal? Standard or more creative? Addressed to HR or to the hiring manager? The rules for writing an effective cover letter are about as plentiful as the rules for writing an effective resume.

I will give you my opinion on what's important in a cover letter. It should be brief, accurate, and directly address what your goal is. Make sure the employer doesn't have to spend too much time reading it (brief), be sure it is grammatically correct (accurate), and states clearly why you think you are suited for the role and that you are interested in being interviewed (your goal.)

A cover letter (like a resume) will not be the instrument that compels an employer to bring a person in for an interview. It can, however, be a tool (like a resume) that an employer uses to weed a person out. In the ideal situation, you have identified an opening via a referral or you have made a personal connection with the hiring company, so there is little need (if any) for a cover letter.

Presenting Yourself Well In Email Communications

Email, as a form of introduction, paints an immediate and very vivid picture of you - good, bad, or indifferent. When you are looking for a job and you want to send an email message that will NOT immediately result in a rejection letter, there are three questions you can ask yourself before you hit the send button.

First, what is the overall TONE of the email? What does your tone say about your attitude? Do you sound negative? Are you complaining? Are you somehow a victim of a bad economy? Will reading your email engage the person reviewing it or repel them? Next, ask yourself if your email message goes beyond "I Need a Job." Are you telling the employer anything about you – besides the fact that you "want a job"? Are you letting them know what attracted you to their web site? Or their company? Or their industry? Or are you simply letting them know about your needs? Remember, companies want to be acknowledged just as much as you do.

Being complimentary to a company representative is just as helpful in getting a job as being complimentary to a stranger can make them a friend. Companies want to find a connection between you and their culture. The only way they'll be able to do that is by learning more about you than the fact that you "need a job." And last, but not least, ask yourself how professionally your email is written. I cannot emphasize the importance of professionalism in the written form enough. The normal informality of email can actually work against you when it comes to making a first impression on a prospective employer. I can't tell you how many emails I receive – from complete strangers, who are basically introducing themselves to me – that contain spelling errors, typos, and sentence fragments. Who is going to be seriously interested in pursuing a working relationship with someone who doesn't even bother to look at what he or she has typed? Do they want someone working for them who doesn't bother to spell-check an email? My guess is no.

Before you send an email, ask yourself this: Would you send out your resume with half sentences, typos or spelling errors? An employer is seeing you for the very first time in that email, and it says just as much about you as your resume would -- maybe even more -- if that email is sloppy or informal. An employer is going to wonder "would that person double-check an invoice/work order/service request before sending it out?" An unpolished email leaves the same impression as if you walked into a room with dirty hands, uncombed hair, unbrushed teeth, or wrinkled clothing.

I believe the very best resume is not the one that impresses the most, but rather the one that offends the least

preparing for the interview

Chapter 14

So now you have your
resume in hand. What does
the successful recruiter do next
to make sure her "Send Out"
becomes a placement?
She prepares her candidate
for the interview.

Preparing A Candidate To "Get The Offer"

In the recruiting business it's called "The Prep." One of the things I learned as a recruiter is that my sale is one of the few sales in which the salesperson is not present during the decision-making or the closing step of the sales process. Think about it. When you buy a house, the realtor is present as you look over the features of the house. He guides you through the home pointing out the pluses and minuses of a particular residence. As he does this, you the buyer are determining if it's someplace you could imagine waking up in and driving home to for the next several years of your life.

Now let's look at the hiring or recruiting process. During the interview, when that sale occurs, the candidate and client are determining if they can live together for the next several years of their lives, and the salesperson (recruiter) is not present. That's right, the product is there (you, the candidate), the buyer is there (the employer), but the salesperson is back in the recruiting office crossing his fingers and hoping everything works out - that is, the employer makes an offer and the candidate accepts the offer.

Good recruiters - which is what I am trying to teach you to become - do their very best to prepare their candidates and clients to close the sale in their absence. Since we're most interested in helping you (the candidate) get an offer, I'm going to talk you through a typical candidate prep. Using these steps to prepare yourself for an interview will put you light years ahead of your competition.

Researching The Company

A recruiter describes the company and the company culture to the candidate as best he or she can. Since you are your own recruiter, it's up to you to do some research on the company. Look on the Internet to find general information on the company, its history, etc. But look deeper for what people are saying about this company. One of the things I discuss with hiring companies before I conduct a search for them is what the word on the street is about them. What are their competitors saying about them? What are their clients (or former clients) saying about them? The company's website will tell you their story from their perspective. Try to get some information from other perspectives, so that you have a complete picture. I have had many candidates eliminated from the running for a position because they skipped this step. <u>Do your research</u>. Talk to people you know about the company. Find out what they are saying. Pull up press releases. Check archived articles from business periodicals or trade magazines. Become educated so you can make a solid career choice and so you can have a higher level exchange of information with the hiring manager.

What Type Of Organization Are You Interviewing With? And Why Does It Matter?

Every organization has a unique culture. But did you know industries also have unique characteristics you can consider as you prepare for your interview? While it's true that in the final analysis, the employer's decision will be based upon common criteria (skills, experience, education, chemistry, etc.) the process to get to the decision can vary depending on the type of company you are interviewing with. Here are some examples:

Corporation – Corporate entities spend millions of dollars developing hiring practices that will increase their odds of attracting and selecting the very best talent to work for them. And corporations (and I know I'm generalizing) are fairly sophisticated in their approach to the selection process. Because most interview "How To" books speak of the interview as conducted by a person working within a corporate setting, as you prepare for an interview in a corporation, you can rely on the tips you'll get from those books. You'll likely be asked behavior-based questions by skilled (or sometimes not-so-skilled) human resources professionals. You'll probably fill out a standard application. You'll most likely be interviewed by multiple people. Finally, the process (in most cases) will be purposefully managed.

What are some characteristics that make these industries unique?

Banking

Advertising

Manufacturing

Research & Development

High Tech

Service

How might the general cultures of these types of industries impact the hiring process?

Foreign-Based Corporation – In the last decade, the Metro Detroit market has benefited by the influx of foreign-based companies. While this has had a very positive impact on the goods and services we produce, the hiring processes employed by companies based abroad vary tremendously from our well-regulated processes. Yes, we all have to abide by the same laws, but you will find yourself answering questions that seem unusual (and sometimes just this side of inappropriate) when you interview with a foreign-based company whose human resources process has not kept up with its manufacturing process. I am not excusing these companies from not following the same guidelines that the rest of the human resources people in the US follow; I am merely acknowledging that this is a new skill for the foreign-based company. And you, the interviewee, need to be prepared.

Entrepreneur – Whereas the corporate interview is often predictable and structured, the person who is interviewing at a smaller, more entrepreneurial organization can expect a completely different interview experience. When I refer to a smaller, entrepreneurial company, I'm talking about a company whose professional staff (the people in the office) numbers under about 20.

These companies' processes are not held as closely accountable to such governmental agencies as, say, the EEOC. Many of these companies lack well-defined Human Resources policies (unless someone has taken it on as a pet project) so the hiring process is left in the hands of well- intentioned, but unskilled personnel. The "How To" books don't usually speak to these interview scenarios directly, but when they make references to things employers should NOT do or questions employers should NOT ask on interviews, they are usually talking about the entrepreneurial interview experience. It is at these interviews that you will need to be prepared to handle questions that perhaps you ought not be required to answer.

Educational Institution – I had the experience of serving on a search committee for the dean of a college within a major university. One might assume an educational institution would naturally have all the know-how when it comes to hiring. After all, educational institutions have access to a huge knowledge bank, right? Well, there is a distinct difference between information *stored* and information *applied*. In my experience the hiring mechanism used in academia isn't the same mechanism used in traditional corporate hiring.

As you prepare for an interview in academia, you'll need to be cognizant of the time it will likely take to complete the process and the diversity of the stakeholders with whom you will meet. These interview processes are extremely elongated, due to the number of individuals who must meet with the candidates, the time involved in gathering feedback, and the reporting of information. Often, labor agreements require extensive background checking, etc.

Next let's consider the logistics and some of the physical realities of preparing to go to an interview:

Where Is The Facility Located?

Do you know exactly where the employer is located? If not, go online for directions. And don't trust our friends at online mapping sites. While their directions are accurate 99% of the time, there is always the possibility that they are not totally accurate or - worse yet - they are articulated in a way that can easily be misunderstood. Take a dry run to the employer's facility to be sure of its location.

Ask If There Is A Specific Entrance To Use

Especially when visiting a larger corporation, it is important to know which entrance to use and what to look for when you get there. Employers appreciate the fact that you are asking this information up front rather than guessing about what you will encounter when you arrive.

Know Who To Ask For

Don't assume that the person with whom you are talking is the person with whom you will first meet. Clear up this assumption by asking the question, "Whom shall I ask for when I arrive?" Why does it matter? Different interviewers have different agendas and needs; therefore, you can mentally prepare for whatever will be coming your way *before* you are sitting in front of the person asking the questions.

Who's Going To Interview You? And What's The Difference?

Let's look at some of the possible individuals you may meet:

An Outside Recruiter

If you are meeting with a recruiter, realize that this person is given the responsibility of weeding out people who are not qualified, so that the hiring manager is spending his or her valuable time interviewing only candidates who are likely to be a fit. So a recruiter will ask many questions like those you would encounter from an internal HR person: What have you done? Where have you worked? What are your skills? Your answers to these questions will allow them to visualize you "doing" the job.

Additionally, recruiters ask questions of candidates to learn about them on a broader scale. They do this in order to potentially consider a candidate for other openings they themselves may be trying to fill (or openings they anticipate trying to fill). As a candidate, you'll encounter this more in a market or industry experiencing high demand for, and low supply of, people with your skills. But even in down times be sure to let a recruiter know *all* about you. Let them know *all* the things you can do and are willing to do, so they can consider you for more than just one opening.

A note about good recruiters: As a job seeker, you are likely to meet a wide variety of recruiters whose effectiveness spans a broad spectrum. You'll meet recruiters who are simply product handlers, who just need a body who is qualified to do a job, who will not treat you with the respect you deserve because their focus is on the prize – the placement – and not on your success. You'll meet recruiters who are not skilled too. Recruiting attracts many people from many industries and disciplines. Many recruiting practitioners have no experience whatsoever in hiring, interviewing, or advancing people's careers.

In your search, you *may* meet with a good recruiter. By a good recruiter, I mean someone who:

Understands the hiring company's goals

Understands your goals

Is committed to a process that results in both parties reaching their goals

Good recruiters know that if they help their clients and candidates get what they want, they will naturally get what *they* want. Bad recruiters (and there are more of them than you can imagine) are interested in getting what they want (a placement) and they will do whatever they need to do to reach that end.

The moral of the story? Get to know the recruiter to whom you are entrusting your career. Make sure he or she has your best interests in mind as he or she represents you. But if you must interact with a less than desirable recruiter in order to be considered for a particular job, be mindful of what his or her motivations may be, and act (or react) accordingly.

Interviewing With Human Resources

Normally, HR is most concerned with what I'll call "matching." HR wants to know if you have the requisite experience, the education, the skills and the ability to fit within their culture. Their first goal is to verify that the information that attracted them to your resume is true and complete. You'll find their questioning following a more linear path. For instance: "Tell me about your experience," "What did you do here?," "What did you do there?," etc. They will focus on "what." They will also spend time on "why" - primarily as they relate to your departures from and arrivals at various positions. You'll hear questions like, "Why did you leave ABC Company?" and "Why did you move to XYZ Company?" Their goal is to provide a clean framework to the hiring manager, free of red flags or inconsistencies. (Remember: HR was traditionally an administrative function, so you can sometimes sense the "check list" mentality of an old school practitioner by the depth of questions they ask.)

For more evolved HR representatives, you'll be asked more than the typical clear-up-any-red-flag-area types of questions. These folks have learned about behavior - based questions, and they will use them to get deeper into their understanding of the candidate: Do you have the right skills and the right experience? From these people, you'll hear questions more like, "Tell me about a situation when you had to deliver an unpopular message to your boss." Sometimes the HR person's goal is to delve deeper into your skills/experience to determine a fit, but oftentimes the goal is to expose information that will lead to a conclusion of whether or not you are a fit for the company's culture. You'll know you're interviewing with an evolved HR professional when you hear questions like, "Tell me about a time that you worked in an organization that was experiencing financial difficulties. How did this impact your relationships with your peers, your superiors, and your customers?"

These questions are a little trickier, so they deserve some thought.

Behavior-Based Interview Questions

In the last two decades, employers have come to realize that simply asking a candidate his or her opinion will not capture the information needed to make a sound hiring decision. Let's take a look at the opinion-based question. It goes like this:

> **Bob, if we were to hire you, how would you turn around the customer service department?**

Or

> **Bob, what's the best way to turn around a customer service department?**

Now, whether or not Bob has ever been charged with the responsibility of turning around a customer service department and despite Bob's ability (or lack thereof!) to do such a thing, Bob certainly has an opinion of how it should be done. But does that mean Bob can do it? Is the employer really learning about Bob's behavior or ability? No, they are just getting a view of Bob's opinion… which, by the way, may be attractive to an employer who is desperate to hire someone.

Behavior-based questions were developed by employers who realized that a candidate's opinion was just that - an opinion. And it had little to do with the applicant's ability to successfully fulfill the requirements of a particular job.

Here are some examples of behavior-based questions:

Describe a time when you were involved in a stressful situation that required you to demonstrate your coping skills.

Give me an example of a time when you set a specific goal and were able to meet or achieve it.

Give me an instance when you had to conform to a policy that you did not agree with.

Tell me about a time when you had to go above and beyond the call of duty in order to get a job done.

Tell me about a time when you had too many things to do and you were required to prioritize your tasks.

Give me an example of a time when you had to make a split-second decision.

What is your typical way of dealing with conflict? Give me an example.

Tell me about a difficult decision you've made in the last year.

Tell me about a recent situation in which you had to deal with a very upset customer or coworker.

Describe a time when you anticipated potential problems and developed preventive measures.

Tell me about a time when you were forced to make an unpopular decision.

Preparing For Behavior-Based Questions

How do you prepare for behavior-based questions? It's not possible to anticipate every question you *could* be asked. But you can prepare by examining what's important. What are the important traits that this particular position might call for? What are the important qualities that this culture might be interested in? What are the important characteristics that this industry looks for? For example, if you are interviewing for a Controller position at a manufacturing company that is just emerging from bankruptcy and has lofty plans for growth, you might be ready for questions like this;

Give me a specific example of a time when you used good judgment and logic in solving a problem with your company's forecasting system. (Important for the job)

Give me an example of a situation where you had to keep people motivated during a stressful time. (Important for the culture)

Explain the strategies you have used successfully to reconcile discrepancies in production numbers. (Important for the industry)

Tell me about a time that you had to initiate a change that was unpopular or that had uncertain results. (Important for the company's plan)

What are some behavior-based questions you need to be ready for, given your background?

Write down some questions an employer might ask you that demonstrate you have what it takes:

To do the job:

To work within this industry:

To work within this culture:

To be a part of this company's future:

Start with   "Give me an example when...

"Tell me about a time...

"Share with me information about...

"Describe a situation when...

Interviewing With A Line Manager

When you meet with typical line managers, they - like HR - will be interested in your ability to complete the task at hand. You will hear questions like;

"Can you do this job?"

"Where have you done this sort of job before?"

"When you did this job before, just how did you do it?"

"Who else did this job with you?"

Their questions will tend to be more specific, because they most likely were promoted to their job from the one you are applying for. So the questions they will ask will allow them to visualize how easily you will fit into their "line" so to speak.

Some more evolved line managers ask questions that are less task-driven and more focused on how you will "fit" within their team. But in my experience, I have found that, unlike, HR, line managers are just not trained interviewers. They haven't mastered the skill of asking open-ended questions that lead you, the candidate, to give answers that expand on your credentials. So, as a candidate you'll need to be prepared to give more information than is asked of you when meeting with a line manager. You'll have to take a more active part in painting the picture of you performing the position they are hiring for. You'll hear things like, "Have you done accounts receivable?" And if you tend toward compliance and non-dominance, your natural answer to this question is, "yes." But if you want the line manager to see you doing the job, you'll need to break out of the compliant/non-dominant comfort zone for a moment and expand on what accounts receivable looked like at the last place you worked. If you really want to bust free of your comfort zone and give the very best answer, I would suggest *asking* a question that will allow you to craft an answer that will give your potential new line manager the information he or she will need to see you in the job.

What does this look like:

"Have you done accounts receivable?"

"Yes, I have. What part of the accounts receivable process would you like me to expand on?"

"Have you done accounts receivable?"

"Yes, I have. Can you tell me how your accounts receivable system is set up here so I can give you some examples of what I've done that sound similar?"

Interviewing With Your Potential Next Boss

In my recruiting experience, I placed executive secretaries who support CEOs, Presidents, CFOs, COOs... top level executives. When the executive secretary meets with this individual, nine times out of ten, she tells me in the debrief following the interview, "you know, he never asked me any questions!" You might think this is crazy for the top level executive to not ask questions, but remember, he or she for the most part is relying on his or her staff (HR, line managers, etc.) to determine capability. The executive, the president, the principal is more interested in the fit from a chemistry and cultural perspective. The nagging question in their mind as they interview you is, "Can I live with you for most of my waking hours?" (chemistry) or "How will you relate to the people within my world?" (fit). Rarely will you hear the CEO ask you technical questions unless you and the executive have the same type of experience. You'll hear more strategic-based questions and less mechanics-type questions.

Interviewing With The Owner/President/Principal Of The Company

Like your potential next boss, these people are most likely more interested in how you fit with the company culture than in your specific skills. These are the big-picture thinkers. These are the strategists. They want to envision you as it relates to their company's future. Their line of questioning (if they choose to ask questions at all) will therefore speak to more attitudinal - or core values-related items.

You might hear questions that start out with:

"What are your thoughts on…?"

"How do you feel about…?"

"Why do you believe…?"

"What is your take on…?"

"What direction do you see…?"

"Where do you see…?"

As we said earlier, your **core values and Life Vision will lead you to the correct answers to these leaders' questions.** And there aren't right or wrong answers. If you don't land a job based upon your answers to these broad-based questions, it doesn't mean you were wrong or the company was wrong. It means you weren't a fit for the company or the company wasn't a fit for you. Remember, **this isn't just about getting any old job.** It's about **finding yourself in a position that is a** *fit for you*.

Interviewing With Your Peers

Many companies like to include the people with whom you will work in the interview process. These companies either want to promote a sense of involvement on the part of the team or they want the team to flush out issues that have gone unresolved in the mind of the hiring manager. Those companies who are engaging the team to foster an atmosphere of involvement look for feedback after the interview from peers that tells whether or not you will blend easily with the team. Conversely, companies whose interviewers are not as skilled may rely on the team to gather information from the candidate via the team, under the assumption that the candidate will be in a more relaxed state when meeting with folks who share the same level of authority or responsibility.

Not knowing what the company's goal might be in any given situation (remember, you are representing yourself, so you don't have a foolproof method of knowing the company's motivation), I would recommend that you recognize that getting too familiar with your potential peers can spell disaster. You are still interviewing, so remember that even your peers are scrutinizing you. I can think of many examples of a candidate spilling her guts about what a jerk her boss was to a peer only to have the peer report back to the potential boss who loses interest due to the conflicting story he heard from that same candidate.

Interviewing Your Subordinates

Much like peer interviews, companies can have a number of reasons for including your potential subordinates in the hiring process. Try to find out what their reasoning might be. <u>Ask what their goal is</u> in having you meet with these folks.

Illegal Interview Questions

As you interview, you will find yourself being questioned by a host of individuals with varying levels of skill and knowledge when it comes to the legalities of interviewing. It is up to you as the candidate to know what can and cannot be asked in an interview. While it's OK to ask for an applicant's name, it is not OK to ask for her maiden name. In Michigan, for example, you can visit the web site of the Michigan Department of Civil Rights where you will find a pre-employment inquiry guide. Check your state for a similar resource.

But how do you get around answering illegal questions? Sometimes these questions are asked by outgoing interviewers who are honestly trying to build rapport with you. In these instances, it may be easier for you to deflect the question.

But how do you answer if a manager comes right out and asks you something like how many kids you have and whether or not you are married?

Don't answer. Ask a question.

Ask, "Can you please explain how my answer to this question determines my qualifications for this position?"

If you wonder if asking such a question could offend the employer, or could cause an employer to eliminate you from consideration for a job, it might. But I would then ask you, is it important that you work for someone who is not only knowledgeable about the law, but is committed to compliance? The answer to that question is yours.

The Courtesy Interview

First of all, I need to clarify one fact: THERE IS NO SUCH THING AS A COURTESY INTERVIEW. I've seen many placements fly swiftly south because my candidate arrived ill prepared or performed poorly because he was told, "I'd like you to meet Jim, the controller. It's just a courtesy interview." It's not a courtesy. Jim may not even want to interview you. The best thing you can do in the case of the courtesy interview is ask a question or two so you can figure out why in the world they've decided to have you meet with Jim. What can you ask? How about, "What will be the goal of my meeting with Jim?" or "What sorts of things should I be prepared to talk with Jim about?" You'll be startled by the amount of information you'll receive that will validate your suspicion that it's not really a courtesy interview.

The Panel Interview

Interviewing with several individuals simultaneously can be an unnerving experience even for the gifted interviewee. There are many books written on how to conduct oneself on a panel interview. You'll read things like: respond initially to the interviewer who asked the question, then as you proceed with answering, acknowledge the other interviewers on the panel by maintaining good eye contact, then as you finish your answer, focus back on the interviewer who asked the question in the first place. And the list goes on.

Try not to get too focused on being perfect. After all, you are in a very unnatural position, and there is a good chance you'll leave something out that you wish you had included. Not to worry, there's always the opportunity to revisit topics in the follow-up process. The most important part of the panel interview in my estimation is the closing. It's the last impression that the group will most likely talk about when you leave. But we'll talk about closing in another section.

The Round Robin/Multiple Interview

In many instances, companies will bring you in to meet with several people in one day. Some companies call it the round robin. You sit in a room, and various individuals are brought into the room to meet with you. While less stressful than a panel interview, the round robin has some inherent frustrations that you can be prepared to meet head on. In some companies where the HR professional understands these inherent frustrations, the interviewers are given specific questions to ask about specific parts of your background. One person will talk about your schooling. Another will talk about your technical skills. One will focus on your work history. And maybe another will talk about your short- and long-term goals. By the end of your interview day, the company hopefully has a clear picture of how you might fit within their organization, and you go home feeling like you worked hard but can still hold your head up. Other companies, who have less structured ways of running the interview process, leave the interview questioning up to the interviewers. And since interviewing is not an inborn talent, they will all tend to ask you exactly the same questions. You'll leave these interviews exhausted and feeling like a broken record. The fourth interview will be much less enthusiastic than the first, and you'll want to die the next time the words, "like I told…" come out of your mouth. But the reality is most of your interviews with several individuals will look like this.

So what can you do? Be mindful that you will be repeating yourself and make a conscious effort to make each version of the same story remain accurate while projecting a consistent level of interest. Remember too, that these interviewers will all meet after you leave and ask one another two questions, "What did you think about him or her?" and "Did he or she seem interested?"

Make sure their answers to these questions are positive.

The Interview Over Lunch Or Dinner

Being interviewed over a meal can be tricky and sometimes intimidating. There are volumes written about some of the subtleties of being interviewed over lunch or dinner or cocktails (although this practice happens much less frequently than in the past), so I will not go into great detail. What I would like you to consider, however, is this:

Interviewing over a meal allows an employer to get to know you better on a more personal level. But don't forget that you are being interviewed! I remember back in the early 80's when I interviewed with a manager at a General Motors plant in Indiana. I was hoping to transfer to this more financially sound division of the corporation. I interviewed with several people in the morning after I arrived and then was taken to lunch by my potential next boss. We talked, ate lunch, and then he asked if I wanted a beer. Of course I did. I was 23 years old and just out of college. Wasn't that what all 20-something budding professionals did? They have a beer with the boss? I had a beer, then I smoked a cigarette, then drove back home to Detroit. A week later got a rejection letter. Imagine that!

Phone Interview

A telephone interview has some distinct advantages and a few inherent disadvantages. First, let's talk about the advantages. When interviewing face to face, you cannot always have all your data spread out before you. But when you are meeting with someone on the phone, you can have all the details about the company, the position, and your credentials readily available. You can even have notes to your self reminding you about how great you are (remember the features and benefits you identified earlier?).

Another advantage of a phone interview is the "friendly turf" reality. Face it, you're in the comfort of you own home where you hopefully feel your best. Even the most skilled interviewee feels slightly anxious or nervous before meeting a potential employer.

But being interviewed on the phone can have its downsides. For one, you cannot always read the interviewer without visual cues. Are they interested in you? Are you giving them enough information or too much information? If you are face-to-face, you can more easily sense how you are being received and make necessary adjustments. Another disadvantage of phone interviews is the possibility of an unexpected interruption on your part that can throw off your concentration. I remember interviewing a potential CEO client on the telephone from my home. I looked out my window and realized my new dog had gotten out of my fenced-in yard. My concentration broken, I tried to silently call my dog back. Had I been in an office, I could have asked to place my client on hold, handled the situation, and returned to the conversation. So do your best to limit distractions that might arise as you prepare for a phone interview. And if at all possible, arrange for the interview to take place at a time you can be in a place with minimal to no potential interruption.

Closing An Interview

A recruiter helps prepare the candidate for the close of the interview. Most applicants are weak in their closing techniques, since closing (unless you're a salesperson) is not an intuitive skill. So a <u>successful</u> recruiter helps the candidate learn how to ask for the job by developing stronger closing techniques.

Here is the typical (weak) interview close:

Employer: Joe, it was very nice to meet you. Thank you for coming in to meet with us.

Joe Applicant: Thank you very much for your time. I look forward to hearing from you.

Ugh! What does that mean? Thanking them for their time suggests that you feel you are somehow intruding rather than adding value to your potential employer's day. And looking forward to hearing from him does not translate into wanting the job. So how can you make your close something other than the same thing everyone else says? How can your closing line be something that demonstrates your qualifications, the fit, your interest, and helps create a solid lasting impression?

Let's try this close:

Employer: Joe, it was very nice to meet with you. Thank you for coming in to meet with us.

Joe Applicant: I enjoyed meeting with you too, and I have one last question for you. Is there anything that you see that could prevent me from being successful in this position?

To which the employer will answer one of two ways.

If the employer says, "No, I don't see anything that could prevent you from being successful in this position," you can then agree and say, "I'd like you to know that I am very interested in coming to work for you (or your organization)."

If the employer says, "Yes, I don't feel that your skills in _____ are as strong as other candidates," you have the opportunity to clarify or restate your skills so the employer has a clear picture of your capabilities. If your skills are still not as strong as others, you now have a realistic picture of your chances of landing this position and can move on to other opportunities.

Either way, you have accomplished a few things with this type of close. You have expressed your interest to your potential employer, demonstrated your confidence in successfully fulfilling the responsibilities of the role, and you have obtained a better understanding of where you fit into the next step in the hiring process.

So now you are clear on what type of organization you'll be meeting with. You know who within the organization you'll be meeting with. You have taken the time to consider all the possible forms of interviews you might participate in. You have considered how you will answer some of the typical interview questions. You've got examples of duties you have performed and goals you have achieved. In a word, you're ready for the interview. But there are still a few items besides your resume that you might need to share with your potential next employer. Next we will talk about what these are and what you need to know about them.

more *things* to prepare for

Chapter 15

Once you are involved with
a company who you think may
hire you, you will likely be asked
for information that will allow
the employer to better
understand who you are
and how you will fit within
the organization. References,
background checks, and work
samples are a few things
that an employer may ask
you to provide.

15

References

At the bottom of most resumes you will find the words "References Available Upon Request" or words to that effect. On most applications for employment you will find sections that ask for references as well. But who should be included among those names? What should you consider when deciding who you'll let vouch for your character to your potential next employer? When should you offer this information to an employer?

First let's consider the right time to provide references. When do you provide references to a potential employer? I have seen resumes that list a person's references including all their contact information right on the resume itself. Remember, the purpose of a resume is to give an employer a snapshot of your experience, knowledge and skills, and is not really an effective tool that will sell you into a position. References, like testimonials, really act as closing devices or tools that help an employer reach a final decision. They aren't "game openers" that serve to get your foot in the door. So *leave names and contact information of references off your resume.*

When is the time right to furnish references? Certainly when an employer asks for them (i.e. on the application or at the interview). But, *if you have not been asked for references by the time your first interview comes to a close, it is appropriate to ask* the employer if he or she would like to contact the people who have volunteered to speak on your behalf.

Whom To Use As A Reference

It's best to use only people with whom you have worked closely as references - a direct boss, a peer, a customer, or vendor. These people have seen your behavior within the context of the work environment, and they are better able to provide the employer with meaningful information. But be sure to talk with these people *before* you give out their names. I am amazed at the number of people I have contacted for references who were surprised by my call. Call your references. Ask them what they feel are your greatest strengths. Ask them what they feel are your weaknesses. Listen to what they say. Are their comments accurate? How will an employer interpret their responses? Will they speak well of your reputation?

Contacting your references before they are contacted by an employer also serves two other purposes. It reinforces to you what your strengths and weaknesses are so that you are better prepared for the time you are asked that question in an interview. And making this connection also builds your relationship between you and the person providing the reference.

Let your references know about the job you are going after. Give them the heads up that they will likely be called to comment on your ability to carry out the responsibilities of that role. If, when you talk with your references, you find they are less than enthusiastic about providing this information or if their presentation of your skills or talents is weak, DON'T USE THEM! Remember, their comments could be interpreted as Law by your potential next employer.

What Can Your References Say About You?

Most sophisticated employers do not divulge much information about former employees other than their dates of employment, titles they held, salary they earned and their eligibility for rehire. Because of the threat of lawsuit, employers over the years have become very tight-lipped about the information they will share about former employees. Still, there are people who, despite their company's policy on reference checks, will share information about you that could potentially hurt your chances of landing a job. And believe me, people like to talk, and these same people LOVE to be asked for their opinions! So when an employer asks for references, think about that.

Background Checks

The Fair Credit Reporting Act states that before an employer can get a consumer report for employment purposes (part of a background check), they must obtain your written authorization. Once you have given your permission to an employer to check into your history, though, they are free to, at a minimum, verify your social security number and, at most, look into your work history, the people you know, your credit history (including your credit payment records), driving records or criminal history. (For example, in Michigan the law allows employers to ask if a person has ever been convicted of a crime or if there are felony charges pending against the person.)

Of course, all employers' inquiries should be related to the job, but to be on the safe side, know what's in your history before you give carte blanche to an employer to investigate you. The best way to prepare for a background check is to be aware of the information an employer might find out about you. Check your motor vehicle record by requesting a copy of your record from the Secretary of State or Department of Motor Vehicles (driving records are not confidential and can be released without your consent). Get copies of your personnel records from your former employer, and make sure the application you completed truthfully states the facts about your departure from an organization.

There are some things employers can not check. School records are confidential and can not be released without your consent. Employers also can not request your medical records, and they cannot make hiring decisions based on an applicant's disability. (They can, however, inquire about your ability to perform a particular job.) And although legally you can't be discriminated against because you have filed for bankruptcy, bankruptcies are a matter of public record – so, since it's easy for employers to attain this information, be prepared.

Credit Checks

Some jobs (especially in industries like finance, banking, etc.) are more likely to require that an applicant's credit history checks out. So get a copy of your credit report. If there is any information on the report that you disagree with, dispute it with the creditor before a potential employer uses it to rule you out.

Internet Checks

The World Wide Web has opened up a big can of worms when it comes to availability of information about you. If you are searching for a job, you need to be aware that anything you put on the web can - and will! - be used to form an opinion about you. And that opinion could mean the difference between you getting an offer and remaining unemployed.

With the popularity of online social networking, candidates are opening up their personal lives – something that historically was not the focus of pre-employment inquiries – to potential employers. So, if you are one of the millions who uses the Internet to communicate with people within your social network, take a look at what image your social and personal profiles are projecting. What does your Facebook page look like? Are there pictures of you on it that promote other than a professional or appropriate image of you? What does your MySpace page look like? If an employer "Googles" you (and I have one client who does this before making any offer of employment), what comes up? What comments have you been posting on other people's blogs and web pages? And what are the blogs you've been posting to? These are all questions you need to ask yourself when you are determining how appropriate your Internet image is.

Letters Of Recommendation

Over the years, I have interviewed hundreds of people who have presented thousands of letters of recommendation. Some are good, and some are not so good. What makes a good letter of recommendation vs. a bad one? Good letters speak to the specific strengths of a candidate and describe a solid working relationship between the candidate and his or her last boss. Bad letters are the ones that are vague, general or - worse yet - quickly put together by the candidate and then signed by the boss.

Work Portfolios

In the world of administrative hires, technical skills and organizational skills are extremely important. There is a strong case for putting together a professional portfolio that includes work samples, letters of reference, awards, certifications, etc. Whether you keep this information in a binder or in a file, the important point is to keep a record of all of your accomplishments and some written proof of the things you've done that you will need to highlight as you interview for a position.

Work Samples - A Word Of Caution On Confidentiality

Many people will provide work samples that will help their potential next employer see the types of projects they have worked on or the technology they have employed at various positions. While this is an extremely effective way to demonstrate your skills, be sure to leave out information not meant to be public. And if there is information in your portfolio that even looks like it might contain confidential information, let the interviewer know you have changed the information to ensure no confidentiality has been breached. I remember one instance where a well-intentioned executive assistant was eliminated from the running on a position because during an interview, she brought forth copies of itineraries she had created for an executive she had supported in the past. The executive who was conducting the interview was very private about his travels and never shared his itinerary with anyone but his assistant. The fact that this assistant shared her former boss's information with him was nothing less than a demonstration of poor judgment. How could this have been avoided? The assistant could have presented an itinerary whose information had been changed (names/dates/times) but could still be used as an example of the method she employed.

So remember, when you are presenting information on projects you have completed (slide presentations, financial projections, strategic initiatives, etc.) <u>look at the information through the eyes of your potential employer.</u> Is there any information that could be viewed as confidential? Is there anything in the information the employer might question? Will they wonder if you should or should not be sharing this information? If the answer to these questions is yes - or even *maybe* - leave the information out of your presentation, or be sure to let the employer know you have modified the information in order to protect the confidentiality of your last employer.

Chapter 16

We've all read the Dress for Success articles that tell us what to wear and what not to wear. In my world of recruitment and staffing, how a candidate presents him or herself on an interview is almost as important as how a bride shows up to her wedding. Now I'm not proposing you spend thousands of dollars on clothing, but I am proposing that you become conscious of what you wear to an interview.

I had the pleasure of speaking
to the viewing audience of a
local TV station, and the host
asked for my guidance on what
a person should know about
what to wear on an interview.
Here are some of the things
I think are important when
you are deciding how to
dress for an interview.

16

The General Rule

For business/professional positions, the general rule on attire is be conservative. Make your interviewer formulate his or her opinion of you based upon your talents and not your attire. In 20-plus years in the recruiting industry, I have never heard an employer say to me, "Great candidate, Therese, but she was too conservative." I have heard other comments about applicants, and they usually start out with, "Did you actually meet with her?" When I hear that question, I know the candidate had probably ignored this general rule.

Know Your Audience

Your audience will determine the appropriateness of your attire. How you dress for a position within the accounting department of a bank, for instance, will be markedly different from how you would dress for an interview for a spot in the creative department of an advertising firm. If you aren't sure who your audience is or what their culture is like, do a little research. Yes… Pick up the phone and talk to some people in the industry.

What You Wear

The business suit is still the standard for an interview within a corporate, executive or professional office. Make sure your suit is freshly cleaned and pressed. It should be up-to-date without being too trendy/flashy, and well fitted/tailored. Remember, you want to feel good in whatever it is you are wearing, but you want the focus to be on you - your strengths, your talents - and not on an ill-fitting suit that makes you feel uncomfortable. Shoes should be polished and in good repair and should again be conservative. (Don't wear sandals, open-toed shoes, tennis shoes, or other shoes that may draw attention.)

Accessories

Accessories should be understated. (Again: draw attention to your skills and experience, and not to your earrings, rings or necklace.) If you have anything but your ears pierced, remove those items before the interview. You can demonstrate your individuality after you land the job. And speaking of individuality and freedom of expression, I'd like to talk about tattoos and piercings. We have all read about the 80 million "Millennials" - you know, the people born between 1980 and 1995. This generation, like the generations of the past, has adopted some habits that bother "older" folks. Like having tattoos. So can you get a job with a tattoo? Yes. Will you be judged negatively by an interview if your tattoo is visible? Possibly. So what are your choices? To that I ask anyone sporting a tattoo this question; What's important? If getting the job is important, cover up the tattoo to avoid the possibility of being judged negatively. If making a fashion or cultural statement is important, display your tattoo with pride. But know there is a possibility that you may be an unemployed champion of tattoos.

How Do You Smell?

The New York Post ran a story about a Brooklyn woman who was fired as a customer service rep because she wore too much perfume. Seem crazy?

Believe it or not, our sense of smell creates an image - positive or negative.
Don't wear cologne or perfume to an interview, as your interviewer could very well be allergic to cologne, or he or she could associate a negative memory with the scent you are wearing. Especially if you are interviewing first thing in the morning, be conscious of how you smell after using your normal hygiene products.

If you are a smoker, do not smoke before your interview. I remember a pretty embarrassing moment I experienced as a recruiter. I was called upon to find an executive secretary for a very successful company. Part of my normal recruiting process involved meeting face to face with the leader of any organization I represented, so I set up a meeting with the President. Of course, being relatively new in the field of recruiting, I was nervous prior to the meeting. All of the typical pre-selling jitters were there: Will they like me? Will they agree to pay my fee? Is this guy a jerk?... So my natural remedy for nerves at that time was to smoke a couple of cigarettes on my drive to the meeting. I arrived, still a little nervous, but able to proceed. The president's secretary met me in the lobby with a smile and a firm handshake, an introduction and then said, "Oh you're a smoker like me!" She was making conversation, but I was mortified! You mean people could actually smell the cigarettes on me? What if she hadn't been a smoker like me? Would I have offended her? I made a mental note to myself: Don't smoke on your way to a meeting, Therese.

And I'll take this smoking thing one step further. If you live among smokers, keep your interview suit separated from the smokers' environment. If you think this is unfair in some way, remember the question: What's important? If getting a job is what's important, put the cigarettes away until *after* the interview.

Coats And Outer Wear

If you are interviewing in the winter, be sure that your outer garments complement the look you are achieving. For example, don't wear a casual jacket or a dated overcoat with a neatly pressed, new business suit. I'll share with you a situation I encountered with a very bright, talented secretary. Her name was Julie. I sent Julie out on three interviews, and she always seemed to end up in second place. I couldn't figure it out. She was skilled, experienced, possessed good communication skills, and presented a nice image. She seemed to have all the right things, but she was always a bridesmaid, and never a bride. I decided to get to the bottom of this. I asked Julie to come back into my office, but to pretend she was going out to meet the actual employer. I waited in the lobby to greet her to see if there might be something in her initial approach that was missing. She walked in. She had on a black leather bomber jacket (this was in 1996 and the jacket was circa 1985) over her business suit. The rest of the picture fit, but the garment she wore over the suit made her look somehow unplanned or uncoordinated. She was emitting a conflicting message, and I believe it was turning off potential employers who were concerned with the image their executive secretary would project.

Colors

Again, the word conservative comes to mind. Don't choose overly bold colors or busy patterns. Remember, you want the interviewer to remember you and not what you are wearing. This reminds me of my first interview with General Motors. Now you have to understand: I come from a blue collar family - Mom was a nurse (they wear uniforms, right?) and Dad was a police officer (uniforms again!) so knowing how to dress for success didn't come naturally. I also didn't have a lot of money to spend on clothes.

I purchased a white (Yes… I said white!) linen suit, then finished it off with a bright red blouse with a flower at the neck. I thought I looked good, in retrospect I must have looked like I was dressed for Easter Mass rather than to interview for my first job in Personnel. Lucky for me, the lady who interviewed me shared my taste in clothes. She even complimented me on my suit!

DO NOT smoke before your interview

Grooming

(Do you think it's crazy that I'm devoting a paragraph to grooming?) In the world of recruiting, I learned that the best recruiters become the best because they leave nothing to assumption. So as far as grooming is concerned, make sure your nails are neatly trimmed and cleaned. Women should avoid having very long nails, or polish that draws attention to them. (Remember, you want the employer to focus on *you!*) Men should be clean-shaven; however, if you are committed to facial hair, be sure your beard or mustache is meticulously trimmed. Hairstyles should be conservative and neat.

This brings up another story. Her name was Bette, and she was interviewing for a position supporting the CEO of a very prominent not-for-profit organization. Her credentials were outstanding, her skills second to none. The HR Director met with Bette, and while he felt she was capable of doing the job, he kept coming back to the fact that her hair was a mess. It looked as though she was caught in a wind storm before arriving and didn't take the time - or didn't feel the need - to straighten out her hair before sitting down to the meeting. Since this CEO needed his assistant to be his "face" to the outside world, the HR Manager was left with the question of whether Bette would understand what a good "face" (and hair) would look like.

presenting

yourself

well

up

paper

wallpaper

Chapter 17

As a job applicant, you will find
yourself filling out a wide variety of
application forms. Many jobseekers
don't consider that these documents
(much like their resumes) can be
tools used to weed them out.

17

Filling Out An Application

I'd like to spend a few minutes discussing applications - and some pet peeves I share with hiring managers. In my recruiting practice, I relied on the application form much more than I relied on the resume. Every candidate was required to complete my application. It was my form; it was my rules. Most candidates complied, although some did not. Thus I got an immediate read on their ability to follow instructions and their willingness to meet some basic requirements of the consultant (me) as well as their potential employers.

You might wonder: why wouldn't someone comply? There are many reasons, and they are unique to each individual. It comes down to either readiness, willingness or capability. By readiness, I mean whether a candidate has adequately prepared for the interview (which, by the way, involves filling out an application). I have heard candidates who fail to completely fill out applications say things like, "I didn't bring all the dates, because I didn't realize I'd be filling out an application." What? You're interviewing for a position with a company, and you didn't think they'd require an application? Do you expect to get a paycheck? **Be ready.**

In my case as a recruiter, I've seen instances where candidates are unwilling to fill out applications (or as I call them, candidate data sheets) because they have some fear or suspicions about how the information will be used. Recruiters run into this with people they interview who are not fully committed to making a job change. These applicants are the tire kickers of the employment world. They think if they don't fill out the application, then you can't somehow take advantage of them. I can remember several interviews that ended in the lobby of my recruiting office because the candidate would not complete the application form.

In some cases, applicants are just plain sloppy, which leads the employer to the conclusion that the applicant is not capable of completing an application. If you can read and write, you should be capable of completing an application in its entirety. Be complete, be accurate and be neat. Yes, employers do look at your penmanship and whether or not you have left off information that should have been included.

Handling Money On The Application

On many company application forms, you'll find a space for "Current Salary" and another for "Salary Desired." The first part (current salary) is fairly straightforward. Or is it? I have interviewed hundreds of people over the years who subscribe to the "inflate-your-current-earnings-because-everyone-else-does" school of thought. I hate to be the bearer of bad news, but everyone else does not inflate their wages. Everyone else puts real world numbers on an application, because they know potential employers will find them out. And guess what? When you knowingly put inaccurate information on an application form, it can be classified as falsification of company records, and that is typically grounds for immediate dismissal. Sound harsh? It's a reality. Put your real current salary on an application form.

Now "Salary Desired" is another thing altogether. Applicants usually fall into a few categories here. One person might assign a very high number to the amount they desire to make, after all, sky's the limit right? Others might sell themselves short because, they just don't see anything "out there" that pays what they really want. And still others listen to their friends and colleagues who encourage them to go for what they are really worth. When I see a number in the Salary Desired spot that looks a little outside of the realm of reality, I ask where the number came from. More times than not, the number was either picked out of the sky or was chosen using flawed logic. My best advice is to write the word "open" or "negotiable" in the spot on the application that asks for the salary you desire. Remember, the salary you desire will depend upon many factors - factors you most likely don't have your head around at the point that you are completing the application. Don't fence yourself in too early. If you put an exact number on the form and it is above what an employer might have in mind, you've just ruled yourself out. Conversely, if you put an exact number on the form and it is below what an employer has in mind, you have just lowered your earning potential and negatively impacted your negotiating stance.

Reason For Leaving

Here's another place that applicants can get into trouble. The trouble usually falls into a few categories: too much information, not enough information, or not the right information. Remember the critical eye of the HR person who ruled out hundreds of people by just glancing at their resumes? This same person is lending that same critical eye to the application form. Don't give him or her a reason to rule you out based upon something you might see as insignificant.

The things that can rule you out generally fall into one of three categories: Too Much Information (TMI), Not Enough Information, Not the Right Stuff.

Too Much Information

I have seen hundreds of applications that contain lengthy explanations (usually in the place that asks for reason for leaving) which create confusion for the person reading the application. An example, "Left because I was subjected to harassment by my manager." A simple "Resigned" would have sufficed. Save the details for the interview. And even then, be cautious about what you share.

Not The Right Stuff

A good example of this is completing the blank that says "Reason for Leaving" with the word "Fired." That's an eyebrow raiser. As they say in my old neighborhood, "Them's fightin' words." When an employer sees the "F" word on an application, he or she is ready with a line of questioning that will no doubt rule you out. Even terminated is a softer word than fired. But remember: Tell the truth. Don't say you were laid off when you were fired. That will be verified in a reference check, and again, falsification can potentially lead to another entry on your application with the "F" word on it.

Not Enough Information

Nothing irritates me more than the applicant who writes "see resume" in the space that asks for job history information. Going back to the previous statement about being ready, willing and capable, I see this as a lack of willingness to comply with a simple request. What makes this applicant think that writing "see resume" makes my job easier?

Let's break it down and look at it from the employer's perspective: I screen dozens or hundreds of applications. I develop a form (the application) that allows me to find information quickly and to consider experience and credentials easily, because everything is displayed in a uniform way. I know where to look for this information, so I can move the candidate along in the hiring process. On one applicant's form I find the words "see resume" where I wished I had found a statement of what he had done to make him right (or wrong) for the opening I'm trying to fill. Now I have to find the resume (which I hope has not become separated from my application form) and I have to search through the resume (which, by the way, is not laid out in a uniform fashion like my form, so I have to spend time looking for what I need to make a judgment) in order to discover information that might be too much or not enough.

Application forms are designed specifically to meet the needs of the hiring company. They ask for exactly the information they need in exactly the amount of space they feel it takes to convey that information. Respect their wishes for information, and don't make their job harder. It's their form. Humor them!

A Word On Penmanship

Yes... People do look at penmanship. This is something I talk about with my 11-year-old daughter. Being the creative, right-brained type of girl she is, Alexa thinks it's OK to write however she wants – regardless of how difficult her words may be to decipher. I have to remind her that penmanship isn't just an expression of her creativity, it's potentially an obstacle to getting her point across. It's also a likely judgment factor in being considered for a position. Even the messiest handwriting can be cleaned up if you slow down and focus on getting your point across legibly.

after the INTERVIEW

Chapter 18

When you leave an interview,
it's important that you reflect on
what worked and what didn't, that
you determine whether *you* want
to move forward, and whether
you think it's likely the
company will too.

18

The first two parts of this process are fairly straightforward: determining what worked and what didn't, and deciding if you want to move forward in the process. The likelihood that the company wants to move forward is not something you can know for certain, but there are ways to determine how likely it is that you will be called back for a second interview or be made an offer.

In coaching, it's called the after-action review. In recruiting, it's the debrief or the pre-close. If you are acting as your own recruiter, do what a recruiter does: debrief yourself (the Candidate) after every interview to determine the "fit." Basically, after you have finished your interview, you need to explore the answers to a few questions:

How effective was the interview?

Am I interested in this job opportunity?

Is the employer interested in me?

How Effective Was The Interview?

What worked? Think about how you felt when you entered the building. How the people there met you. What were your initial reactions? How did the environment compare with the ideal environment you developed when you designed your ideal position? Think about the interview itself. How did you feel as you met with each person individually?

What didn't work? What did you notice in the environment that did not fit within your definition of the ideal position? Were there things in the environment that were a potential turn-off to you? Were there parts of the hiring process that seemed not to flow? Was this a function of you or your preparation? Or was it a function of the employer's interview skills or preparedness?

What would you do differently? Everyone has left a conversation, a meeting or an interview at one time or another thinking, "If I only would have…" What were your "If I only would haves" during this interview? Were there questions that stumped you? Or questions you wished you had answered differently or more completely? Were there examples you thought of after the interview that you wished you could have provided to demonstrate your capabilities more clearly? Did you forget to tell the employer you were interested? Or were there questions you had that you failed to ask? This part of the self-debriefing is usually easy for us, since we are always our worst critic. But let it flow. By acknowledging your shortcomings, you present yourself with a great opportunity to improve your interviewing capability.

Negotiating Salary: What Works? What Doesn't Work?

One of the most anxiety-inducing stages of the interview process is the negotiation of your salary. I wish I had a nickel for every time I heard the question, "How should I handle money?" or heard the statement, "I hate talking about money!" Salary negotiation does not need to be intimidating, if you look at it as a fact-finding mission and if you give yourself the time and space to respond to the employer.

Here is a typical scenario.

The potential employer asks, "How much are you willing to accept?" or a bolder employer might even ask, "What's the least you would accept?"

Resist the temptation to throw out a number. Why? You have a 50% chance of shooting too high and a 50% chance of shooting too low. Let's say you made $50,000 at your last job, and an employer asks you the question, "How much are you willing to accept?" If you're unemployed, you might be tempted to say, "Anything! I need a job!" or you might say, "I'd like to make $50,000."

What if the employer was thinking of $49,500? You've just ruled yourself out!

What if the employer was thinking of $55,000? You've just lost $5000!

So how do you answer? Let an employer know how much you made in your last job. (Often, this is really what they are asking for.) But then let them know that you are interested in their best offer. This accomplishes two things: it allows an employer to see where your salary fits as compared to other candidates and their current wage structure and it demonstrates that you are open to discussing (or negotiating) other options.

Now let's take this a step further. Let's assume the employer throws out a number. If it sounds great, then take it! If it sounds good or even not so good, handle it this way: Say, "That sounds great, and I would like to seriously entertain your offer, however, may I have a day to consider it?" This gives you the space to leave the interview, review all the details in whatever depth you like, and then come back to the employer with either your acceptance or a counter offer.

A Recruiter Closes The Candidate

What this means is that a recruiter finds out if the candidate is ready to move forward and accept an offer of employment. So is your MPC ready for the close?

Here are some questions a good recruiter asks a candidate after an interview:

If they were to make you an offer of $_____ would you accept it?

Is there anything that would prevent you from accepting an offer?

When are you available to start?

What other offers do you have pending? And how do they compare?

Are You Interested In This Job Opportunity?

What is your interest level? It's tempting for someone who is unemployed to fake a high level of interest just to get the job. You fool the employer into thinking you want the job at the interview, and then you fool yourself into thinking you want the job after the interview just to secure a paycheck. But let's pretend for a moment that you are currently employed, you don't *have* to take a job, and you will only take a job that is suited to you. How interested in the job are you - really? Want to do a quick check to test your interest? Ask yourself this question:

What are the top three reasons I am interested in this job:

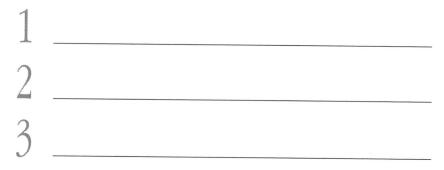

1 _____

2 _____

3 _____

If reason #1, 2 or 3 is "because I need a job," the recruiter in me would question whether or not you are really interested. This is a critical part in the process for a recruiter. It is at this time that the recruiter is testing motives that lie beneath the surface. Good recruiters won't move a candidate forward unless the candidate can sell them on two things: first, that the candidate is truly interested and motivated to accept an offer and second, that the candidate's reasons for being interested in the position line up with what they indicated their priorities were in the first place. If there is a misalignment, the recruiter will need to uncover the reason for it to protect his or her client from making an unwise hiring decision. As your own recruiter, you can give yourself the acid test just as a search professional would. If you forgot what was important in your ideal job, look back to your priorities you listed in Chapter 8.

In my opinion, this is the most critical point in the closing process and one of the greatest values a recruiter brings to their clients: Not allowing a placement to happen that should not happen.

Is The Employer Interested In Me?

How can you figure out if the employer is interested in you without them coming right out and saying, "Hey, I'm really interested in hiring you!" Let's examine what you, as a recruiter, would want to know. What information will your "inner recruiter" need to gather to determine if the process will move forward?

Here are some questions to ask yourself:

How long was I at the interview? Sometimes the length of time an employer spends with you indicates his or her level of interest. Sometimes, though, it can simply indicate the level of the interviewer's time management skills or countless other "non-candidate-related" factors. Still, consider the time the employer took to explore what's important to you and how the company or the opportunity may meet your needs.

With whom did I meet? The recruiter will want to know all the people you met. Did you meet your potential boss? HR? Peers? Subordinates? If you only met with HR, it's likely you'll need to go back again. If you met with HR, line management, the President, and your potential coworkers, you may not need to go back. And it would appear that the employer has a genuine interest in moving you forward in the process given the amount of human resources they invested in meeting with you.

What was discussed? What sorts of things did you discuss with each person? The job? The company? The person's background? Your background? Personal items? Again, a recruiter wants to understand the depth and breadth of the conversations. While you will not have a point of comparison as a recruiter has - remember, a recruiter usually sends more than one candidate - reflecting on your discussion will help you identify items that would point to the employer's interest level.

What sorts of questions were asked? Were you asked behavior-based questions? Were there any questions that stumped you? Did some people ask you the same questions? How do you feel you did in answering the questions? Is there anything you wish you had said that might impact the employer's interest in you?

Did you fill out an application? Some employers will have a person fill out an application upon arrival at the interview, and some employers will have a candidate take the application home and return it at a later date. Did the employer ask you to fill out other pre-employment paperwork? Physical, drug-screen or background information forms? Does the employer give these forms to everyone they meet? Or does the fact that they gave you the forms indicate a serious interest in you as a candidate? Is it possible to ask this?

How was it left? The common mistake candidates make is that a friendly good-bye from potential employers means they are interested in them. What was said in closing? Did they ask you to return for another interview? Did they outline their next step or did they simply thank you for your time? Did they say they have other candidates to interview? Did they ask you when you can start? Don't assume the interview went well just because you heard a cordial good-bye.

Following Up: What Is Your Next Step?

You have already asked the employer what the next step is, and hopefully you received an answer. What type of follow up might be necessary? Let's explore some of the possibilities:

Scenario #1: Employer says you are one of the first people to interview, so the next step is to bring back candidates for a second interview.

Scenario #2: Employer says they will be finished with the final interview process by a specific date.

Scenario #3: Employer says they will begin the reference checking process.

Scenario #4: Employer says they will need you to do something (complete a task, respond to an inquiry) within a specified period of time.

Scenario #5: Employer says they will be in contact with you after a specific event or date.

The only way to determine your next step is to ask questions that allow you to see where the employer is headed. It is completely acceptable to ask about next steps. And notice I said next "steps" and not next "step." In my recruiting training, one of the valuable skills I employed was the ability to ask questions that led to the end of the process and not just to the next step. My goal was to understand the entire process, and to have a mutual understanding with my employer on how things would flow between now and the time someone was seated in the vacant chair. Let me give you an example of a possible end-of-interview scenario that will get you, the candidate, to the end of the process in the eyes of the employer:

Candidate:	What is the next step in the process?
Employer:	We will be calling our finalist candidates back for second interviews.
Candidate:	When will second interviews happen?
Employer:	Most likely by next week.
Candidate:	Great, after the second interview, if things go well, will you be in a position to make a decision?
Employer:	No, we'll need to bring people back a third time to meet the CEO.
Candidate:	Oh, so realistically I could expect to return two more times. Would it be safe to assume that a decision would happen after that meeting?
Employer:	Well, we'd need to do reference checks and background checks.
Candidate:	Can I get you any information that will assist you in that process?
Employer:	No, I have everything I need on your application.
Candidate:	Great, I'm very interested. Once those references are complete, is it normal to present an offer at that time?
Employer:	Yes.
Candidate:	Well, again, I'd like you to know that I am very interested in returning again to meet with your staff and CEO.

Now realistically you may not have to go that far, but do you see what happened here? The recruiter (you, the candidate) did not fall into the trap of making assumptions about what's going to come next. This scenario may be a little involved, but I want to demonstrate the point that if you hadn't asked any questions, you could very well have left thinking the employer would be making an offer in a few days and would call you. In this scenario, where two more interviews were required, and reference and background checks were needed, you would be anxiously waiting for a call that simply wasn't going to come in the timeframe you expected. By asking the questions you eliminate the assumptions, and you come to an understanding of the process, so your expectations of a call back are based on reality. In the example, if you had asked the questions, you'd know that it is very likely you will not hear from this employer for one to two weeks depending upon the number of applicants they are considering. You can use this one to two weeks to turn other job leads into interviews rather than sitting at home waiting for something to happen that simply isn't going to happen. Or worse yet, you can let all the self-doubt creep into your consciousness that says, "They must not want me, or they would have called." No, they may want you, but they just have to go through the process you assumed you understood. Don't waste your energy on pining over false assumptions.

Sending A Thank You Note

It is common practice to send a thank you note to an employer after you have been interviewed. What should you consider when you are crafting a thank you note?

Your interest level – Are you really interested in the position? If so, send the thank you. And be sure to let the employer know exactly why you are interested within the context of your note. Remember: Employers want to be wanted just as much as you do.

What form to use – Think about whether you should use a more formal or informal tone with the employer. Should you send the follow up via email or via regular mail? Should you send a different note to all the people you met, or send one email to the highest-ranking interviewer and copy (cc) the others?

Details to include – Is there anything you feel you did not get across during the interview regarding how well you fit? Were there skills you did not highlight? The thank you note can be a way to provide the employer with details that will give them the complete picture of you.

When to send – There are several schools of thought on the timing of sending a thank you. I would recommend sooner rather than later; however, if you are working with a recruiter, hold off sending the note until after you've received feedback from the recruiter. It is possible he or she will find out information you can incorporate in the note that will, again, allow you to give the employer a more complete picture of you.

Conclusion

For 20 years, I have observed the job-seeking habits of thousands of people. I have participated in the successful job searches of thousands of candidates whom I have placed. The common denominator in all of the success stories is "Action." The people who land a job even in the crummiest of all economies are the people who take action. The people who don't wait for things to "turn around." The people who don't go at things the same way they always have. The successful job seekers are the ones who consider the possibility that there is a better way to land a job. They consider the possibility that there are jobs out there if they just take a look at an old picture using a new and refined lens.

I hope these pages have given you some ideas that you can use – that you can put into action. I hope you will choose to apply a few of the principles I have shared so you can experience different results in your job search. But in any process, the trick is not just learning the principles, but making them a part of your everyday life. Reading this book is the first step, but how do you make it stick?

It Takes Support

You make your learning stick by putting in place some type of support system. It might mean hiring a coach. It might mean joining a job search support group. It might mean connecting with a career counselor, or maybe setting up meetings with a mentor. Whatever you do, enlist the help of someone you respect, who can give you objective support and feedback as you search. You are going to bump into obstacles. And often times, those obstacles will be you! As you move forward in your search, be sure to check in regularly with your support system so those people can help you recognize when you are getting in your own way, and so they can also encourage you when you are doing things right.

Finding a job is a job. And it is a process. By using the tools that are available and tapping into the people who can support you, you are well on your way to landing a job - even in a crummy economy!

I wish you the very best in your search.